A Conscript
for Empire

A Conscript for Empire

The Experiences of a
Young German Conscript
During the Napoleonic Wars

Philippe

as told to

Johann Christian Maempel

LEONAUR

A Conscript for Empire: the Experiences of a Young German Conscript During the Napoleonic Wars
by Philippe as told to Johann Christian Maempel

Originally published in 1826 under the title
The Young Rifleman's Comrade

Published by Leonaur Ltd

Text in this form and material original to this edition
copyright © 2008 Leonaur Ltd

ISBN: 978-1-84677-446-1 (hardcover)
ISBN: 978-1-84677-445-4 (softcover)

http://www.leonaur.com

Publisher's Notes

The opinions expressed in this book are those of the author
and are not necessarily those of the publisher.

Contents

To

His Excellency Freyherrn von Göthe
Minister of State To His Royal Highness
the Grand Duke of Saxe Weimar, &c. &c.

Sir, I do not know any name so well calculated to grace the dedication-page of this interesting little volume, as that under the sanction of which it has been introduced into German literature. In this persuasion, I am not only influenced by a sense of appropriateness; but also feel happy in having an opportunity of expressing the respect and admiration which I have long entertained for your splendid talents and high character.

The fame of the Author of Faust has not been confined even to the numerous divisions of Germany: it has penetrated every portion of civilized Europe; therefore, I am desirous (in common with natives of many other countries) to consider Göthe rather as the Citizen of the World, than of any particular part of it. Your genius and accomplishments, admitted by your countrymen to be pre-eminent, and which will unquestionably render the works of your pen immortal, have ensured their introduction into my native land, which I am happy to say boasts a closer intellectual affinity than any other to your own;—a fact proved, in a great degree, by the endeavours of several of our highly distinguished literati to render into the English tongue the most valuable productions of German inspiration,—as well as by the popularity of the names of Göthe, Schiller, Wieland, &c, amongst the reading classes of my countrymen.

The high regard of the English people for your Excellency's individual merits has been already fully expressed in a variety of ways,—more particularly in the works of our Byron, Scott, Gower, Shelley, and other well-known names. For myself, an humble gleaner in the harvest of British literature, I am proud to offer this little testimony of correspondent feeling, not so much in the character of an individual, as of a citizen of England;—in which light I trust Your Excellency will be pleased to accept it, and to permit me to subscribe myself,

With great respect,

Your Excellency's most obedient servant,

The Translator

London

October 12th, 1826

Editor's Preface

There is a saying amongst us, that fortune is spherical; and I think there is some truth in the adage; since this comparison may be used in another sense besides the common one. The form of a sphere appears to the observer that of a complete, perfect, self-existent figure; and in like manner as its unvaried outline proves unattractive to our eye, so does the smooth course of the fortunate man fail to command our interest.

The state of well-being and contentment is simple and uniform, whatever the source from which it springs. We feel no excitement in dwelling on the contemplation of such a lot; and when, at the end of a drama, the hero and heroine are united, curiosity expires, and the spectator willingly returns home, however powerfully his attention might have been previously enchained by the intricacy of the plot and the distresses and embarrassments of the characters. Untoward circumstances, on the other hand, may be compared with the figure of a polygon, whose numerous angles, by confusing, excite the vision. Its surface is various, broken, irregular. Upon that of the sphere the light seems invited to repose, while those parts not presented to it rest in tender shadows:—the polygon, on the contrary, upon every angular division, exhibits a different tint—a different degree of colouring or of shade; thus amusing the organs of sight, which are busied with the endeavour to comprehend and harmonise the whole. This little volume is calculated to illustrate these considerations. Its contents, with a few exceptions, treat of misfortune, of pain, and despair.

Recitals of this nature are useful and consolatory. Knowledge is always advantageous: therefore we are indebted to those who, having suffered so much,—having had death more than once before their eyes,—have related to us these sufferings, and the manner in which they were redeemed from them; and the reflection is consolatory, that this redemption proceeded from themselves. It is true, indeed, that the exertions of steadfast, active, prudent, humane, and religious men are favoured by the influence of a higher power; and the moral government of the world is presented in its clearest manifestation by assistance afforded to the good and brave sufferer.

The social organization of the exiles of Cabrera, the poorest of the Balearic Islands, cannot fail to obtain the commendation of all thinking men: it exhibits, indeed, an absolute model of a political condition of society, conformable with reason and nature.

The fortitude exhibited, and the struggles made by the unfortunate sailors who were stranded upon a barren rock upraising itself in the middle of the ocean,—evince, in like manner, a model of natural and moral resolution—of native and tried constancy—of considerate and prudent boldness. These men are rescued, by conduct of this description, from a situation the most appalling; and they subsequently meet with others who have encountered similar perils.

What a lesson is thus read to us! and how desirable is it for each individual and unimportant man to see what has been achieved by others equally obscure with himself;—to perceive that they have attained to praise and commemoration simply by the exercise of those virtues, the use of which would be equally necessary in him, should he ever be called to contend with danger and fate!

Thus, I really conceive it to be a work of benevolence to recommend to others the perusal of a book which has suggested such reflections to my own mind; and I trust, that in the heart of every thinking reader, it will sow the seeds of a similar harvest.

Göthe

Weimar, 14th January, 1826

Translator's Preface

Memoir writing—at least that kind of memoir-writing to which the present work belongs, is new in Germany, and sufficiently rare amongst ourselves. It is extremely interesting in its nature, tending of course to make the reader much better acquainted than he could possibly become through any other medium, with the actions, as well as peculiarities of character, of the individual described.

It is curious enough to compare the rarity and recentness of the military adventures we possess, with the great importance of the subject, and the moderate quantity of talent required in its treatment. Military officers are gentlemen; and moreover they are at least supposed to be qualified by education to put together words and sentences according to the received usages of the English tongue. The days of the Ensign Northingtons in Tom Jones are over. If any military man chooses merely to narrate his adventures,—the " moving accidents" which every officer is sure to have encountered in his life-time, as well as "hair-breadth scapes i' th' imminent deadly breach"—if he details these unaffectedly and plainly, and presents the reader with any thing like a faithful picture of his own feelings, the book is sure to be an amusing and interesting one. It is rather surprising, therefore, that the books of this description with which we have been presented since the close of that great struggle which has changed the face of all Europe, have been so few—and especially that it should have been left to persons in the inferior ranks of the army to give us the few we have. Count Rapp has indeed recently published a Narrative of his military life, comprising a striking account of Buonaparte's Expedition to Moscow: but for the grand panorama of that great man's battles, we must look to "the general camp, pioneers and all"—especially to the very entertaining volume lately published in England, entitled, Adventures of a French Sergeant. The still more recent publication, Adventures of a Young Rifleman, between which volume and the present there is a conformity of interest arising from the similar rank, and acquaintanceship, of the respective heroes, shows that the German officers are not more anxious for literary reputation than our own: and a few other personal narratives which have appeared among them, and with which the public may soon perhaps become acquainted, render it manifest that in Germany, as here, the officers have been indebted for some of their fame, as well as their fortunes, to the common soldiers who fought under them.

Even in France, that land of memoirs and memoir-writing, this class of narratives has by no means been abundant, in spite of the tempting effects to be produced from a display of the ever-shifting scenes in the great drama of the Revolution, and the more brilliant, though equally various display of the pride, pomp, and circumstance of war and conquest which succeeded it. There has been nothing published in France, during the revolution, at all equalling in interest or power the Memoirs of Colonel Hutchinson by his wife—the personal narrative of Captain Crichton, printed in Swift's Works; or even Defoe's History of a Cavalier, which he compiled from the floating military reports and traditions of his time. The works in France that come nearest these in character and interest are undoubtedly the memoirs relating to the struggle in La Vendée—especially that which bears the heroic name of Larochejaquelin: but even these memoirs, delightful and various as they are, want the charm of variety, of change of scene and manners, which is perpetually giving its gay and shifting colours to the story of a life of restless and predatory adventure.

All this will be met with in the Rifleman's Comrade, which has found an Editor whose fame is even more extensively European than the adventures of the hero. This celebrated leader in the republic of letters has already stated, in his own Preface, the principal materials whereof the present volume is composed; which bear, in some of their features, as we have already hinted, a family resemblance to those which have already obtained a great share of popularity under the title of The Young Rifleman, to which work the present was published in Germany as a companion.

The reader will be tempted to smile, now and then, at the national prejudice displayed by the author of the following narrative:—"the good German manners,"—"the temperance and industry common in Germany,"—"the honest and social feelings characteristic of his native country," brought by the German colonist to Port Louis,—all these expressions savour strongly of that esprit national which we should almost have thought so general an acquaintance with the world would have eradicated from the writer's mind.

His observations on men and things, with the exception of the Spaniards, in treating of whom he exhibits a prejudice similar in its nature to the foregoing, although of a complexion widely different, appear to be at once fair and sensible; and sprinkled, here and there, with a latent spirit of humour which renders them occasionally very piquant, relieving pleasantly the deep and tragic nature of the general interest of the story.

After all, we are at a loss to know how much of this book may belong absolutely and bona-fide to the illustrious writer by whom it has been introduced to the world. With regard to the eloquence displayed in various parts, that is not much to the purpose; since of course the style would receive a tinge from the glowing imagination of the Editor: but it must be confessed that, at times, the elevation of sentiment and refinement of taste displayed by the Rifleman seem somewhat beyond the sphere of his alleged rank. This is, however, mere guesswork; and refers, at most, to the speculative portions of the volume:—the facts narrated bearing throughout the unequivocal stamp of individual truth and reality.

A slight freedom has been in one or two instances taken with the text, but in no matter whatever of importance. The translator has sought rather to render the spirit and gist of the original than to adhere to it literally: here and there, also, an expression has been suppressed, on account of the established difference of taste between the two countries.

Chapter 1

Conscripted

I was born during that eventful period when the horrors of the French Revolution resounded throughout Europe—a period which must remain indelibly impressed on the imagination and memory of all those who were its contemporaries. My father was a respectable butcher, and was elected mayor of the small town in which we lived. My education was as good as the troubled circumstances of the time admitted it to be. Among other indications of these circumstances was the fact, that our priests were not permitted to exhort publicly: nevertheless, the good work was not left unheeded; they came in the night-time into the houses of their penitents, and sought to impart that consolation and courage so necessary under the pressure of adverse events. I need scarcely say that the general habits of the people were not of the purest description, at a time when trees of liberty sprang up like mushrooms, around which the furious Jacobins danced and roared to the melody of their *ça ira*. A great many things were exhibited to the unpractised eyes of youth by no means consonant with those feelings of modesty and shame so amiable in the juvenile disposition.

I can remember very well that my father was taken one night out of his bed, bound, and conveyed as a prisoner to Strasburg. This violence was committed on the plea of his being an aristocrat. He yielded with firmness and patience—replying to the insults of the men who apprehended him with mildness, and expressing his reliance on the divine protection.

Our constancy was not of this heroic description: we were dissolved in tears; we held the knees of the heartless gens d'armes, and implored them not to deprive us of our protector: but our appeal produced in them only savage laughter and low-bred mockery. They diverted themselves with the excess of our affliction; and when my unoffending parent was removed from his house upon a wheelbarrow, an expression of malicious joy was visible in the countenances of several of our neighbours, which filled his affectionate heart with dread and apprehension on our account.

The national guards had scarcely quitted the house, when a party of sans-culottes forced themselves into it. By these ruffians every moveable thing was abstracted or destroyed. No one dared to interfere in our behalf. The house of one, said to be a friend of the king, was, as it were, confiscated, and it was put into the power of every good patriot to commit in it whatever devastation his benevolence dictated. A little while after came the new mayor, who drove us altogether out of our dwelling, thus compelling us to relinquish the shelter of our paternal roof, utterly destitute of any other asylum or the means to procure one. That man who should have received us would have been marked and proscribed: he would have been set down as an aristocrat, and shared the unhappy fate of one.

A plan was concerted for us to repair to a relation of my mother, who resided on the other side of the Rhine, near Manheim. But the question was, how to get there?—without passport—without money—without bread! My eldest brother, a youth of sixteen, who, having exercised the business of our father, was well acquainted with the country, inspired us with courage, and promised to get us safely over the Rhine, in spite of the watchful diligence of the officers of the customs. I, the youngest and feeblest, was sometimes led, sometimes carried, by my brothers; and thus our progress towards the river was very slow, although it was only four or five German miles distant.[1] In fact, during the day, we were compelled to remain in the forests, sub-

---

1. Five English miles form one German mile.

sisting on the precarious bounty of the neighbouring villagers, which was solicited for the common benefit by my sister and my second brother; my poor mother could only travel at a lingering pace, and I hardly at all; and the third night had arrived when our little forlorn party found itself on the bank of the Rhine.

My eldest brother had separated from us, in order to seek the readiest means of passage, a point of meeting having been previously decided on. Mine was the only heart which did not thrill with anxiety at this period. The shadows of life had not as yet dimmed the sunshine natural to it. I was happily ignorant of the perils by which we were environed; and with plenty to eat, was content and cheerful.

Having reached the spot agreed on, we concealed ourselves as well as possible, and awaited the arrival of our youthful guardian. An hour beyond the specified time elapsed, and still he came not. The whole party was nigh frightened to death—at least with one exception—that of myself, who, as I have already observed, was unable to comprehend the nature of our situation—marvelling why we returned not home, and why we were travelling in the dark night.

At length, the concerted signal was heard, hope revived, and each individual earnestly longed to hear the well-known accents of my brother. He had not been able satisfactorily to fulfil his scheme, which was to take one of the many small fishing-boats constantly lying on the shore. They had all been too well secured; until at last he had met with one in a wood, which he had been obliged to carry a long way to the river: "and after all," said he, "it is scarce fit to receive so many persons; but by God's help, and the use of a pair of tolerably robust arms, I will convey you safely to the other side." It was of little consequence, wanderers as we were, at what point of the opposite shore we might land.

Eagerness to depart was now the prevalent feeling. To have been intercepted at the moment when our redemption appeared so near, would have been doubly grievous. We proceeded towards the river, with strained nerves and in silence,—fear urging our steps, and imparting to us an unwonted principle of strength.

Shortly the rush of the impetuous Rhine became perceptible to our ears. We soon stood upon the shore, and saw the frail bark which was to waft us from a land of anarchy and carnage to one unstained with the blood of kings. The sight inspired us with fresh courage, but it was un-enduring; for a second glance proved how well grounded my brother's apprehensions were as to the capacity of the boat; and scarcely had one of our party set foot in it, when dread of exchanging the hard-heartedness of man for the yet more merciless wave, restrained, with an involuntary cry, the others from following.

This irresolution was combated by my brother with all his eloquence. My mother was the most timid; but at length, even in her, the fear of immediate death was surmounted by that of losing her children: she entered the boat; and my brother pushed from shore. The passage was not without danger, for our boatman was inexperienced: the exigency of the circumstances, however, inspired him not only with fortitude, but with tact. He instructed us all to lie down, himself remaining upright. Thus he relieved himself from harassing observations or ignorant fears, since we knew not the progress of our brief voyage: neither would he answer any question, devoting every energy unencumbered to the reaching with safety the peaceful shore of Germany. At length, his cry of pleasure aroused us, and almost at the same moment we felt our boat push against the sand: we arose, and saw, at the distance of about twenty steps, the desired country.

A brief time sufficed to set us ashore, and fervently did we thank the benevolent God who had thus far preserved us. My brother being known in these parts, we experienced no difficulty in finding our relations, by whom our reception was exceeding friendly, and we obtained, in one way and another, a sufficient provision.

My brother made excursions, at several different times, into France, for the purpose of collecting intelligence touching the condition of my father. These endeavours were, however, in every instance fruitless; nor was this much to be wondered at, since he was obliged to conceal his presence there from public observation, and our true friends could give him no tidings of the fate of that victim of persecution.

In this manner about a year and a half passed away, at the expiration of which period we received a letter informing us that my father had not been convicted of aristocratism, but notwithstanding still remained in close confinement. This news, on the face of it, seemed dreary enough, and yet we all derived hope therefrom. He was still alive. The very arrival of the letter appeared indicative of good, particularly to the longing ardour of my excellent mother, who had suffered severely. I have already said, that we had sufficient for our support; but this sufficiency was derived principally from the Christian charity of the humane neighbours. My brother, indeed, having been engaged as assistant by a butcher, contributed his quota to our sustenance.

One evening (how perfectly it lives in my remembrance!) we were sitting round the fireside: the wind was up, lashing forward the torrent of the Rhine, and huge black clouds were discharging from their heavy masses a deluge of rain, when we heard, quite suddenly, a knocking at the door. It was opened; and, O the joy! my dear father entered. We were mute, from the quick and overpowering revulsion of habitual fear and delayed hope: nor was it until blinding tears had given a passage to our emotion that we were enabled to speak a single word. But then, when the unlocked voice resumed its utterance, how fondly were its powers lavished on the stranger! What a store of endearing expressions! What an infinity of questions, scarcely waiting for reply! The best place by the fire; was awarded to the beloved object of our solicitude, and happiness sat at the heart of every member of our humble circle. After rest and refreshment, my father commenced his story:

You know, that I was carried on a wheelbarrow, like the meanest criminal, to Strasburg. I was insulted, not only by the men who escorted me, but by the greater part of the inhabitants of those places through which we passed; nevertheless there were not wanting many faces lighted up by the divine feeling of compassion. At Strasburg, I was immediately thrown into prison, where I found a great many other unfortunates circumstanced in a similar way. In this state of durance, I continued four weeks without any question being put to me. The Court of Justice (alas, miscalled so!) assembled every day. Most of the prisoners were convicted, few only discharged. At first, the expectation of certain death was fixed in my mind; but by degrees, hope grew up, strengthening itself day by day from the consideration that, had they meant to go to extremities with me, I should have been sooner summoned before their tribunal, as they professed themselves to be furnished with proofs of my pretended guilt. At last my day came round, and I was conducted to the court. With serene face and approving conscience did I go to meet my accusers and judges, for my heart bore me witness that I had demeaned myself as a blameless and good citizen both in the days of the monarchy and in those of the republic. The information against me was read. I was accused therein of having harboured friends of the king and assisted their flight out of France. I could not exculpate myself in this point, because, you know, a great many unfortunate royalists had been assisted by me. I knew not what to say. They demanded my defence: upon which I desired the particular facts to be pointed out, and their proofs adduced. These proofs, as I suspected, they were unable to produce, my caution having been uniformly excessive. A number of captious questions were subsequently put to me, to each of which my answer was concise, often monosyllabic,— yes or no. I never was summoned before the court again.

I beheld neither friend nor acquaintance during the whole term of my imprisonment. This day se'nnight I received my discharge, and hastened home; but, to my inexpressible consternation, found not you, its chief treasures: strangers occupied our dwelling, and you, I was told, had escaped. I lost no time in providing myself with a passport, that I might be enabled to seek you; and here, dear friends, we are met again. All worldly property we have lost, at least for the present: but I trust, by aid of the divine Providence which has given us back to one another, we shall yet see a renewal of prosperous days.

Such was the recital of my father, by which we were all animated with fresh courage. We had again amongst us our revered head and protector. It was in our power to return fearlessly to our native country. The reign of terror had passed; Robespierre, and his deists, were dead or dispersed; and a milder government had superseded their system of horror and atrocity.

After the interval of a few joyful days, my father and brother went home, to try to recover a part of our lost fortune. This separation cost us much inquietude. They departed, accompanied by our hearts' best wishes. We followed them with our eyes as long as the organs of vision would avail us; and when we had quite lost sight of them, turned aside to weep—but not such bitter tears as those which ensued upon our first sad parting.

When the arrival of my father was known in the little town, a general sentiment of joy appeared to prevail. Almost every body came to congratulate him; and no one came with empty hands. Each brought a present—a lesser or a greater one, according to the power of the donor.

After some weeks, our two cherished friends recrossed the Rhine, and apprised us that they had purchased our house for a small sum; and although my father had not the ready money necessary to complete his bargain, the party with whom he had to deal expressed a willingness to trust, as he said, to his honest face.

Having packed together every thing which we could call our own, we took leave of the good-natured inhabitants of the country, thanked them for the abundant proofs they had exhibited of friendship and benevolence, and departed with a mingled feeling of pleasure and pain. We soon stood on the bank of Germany's watery frontier; and easting a retrospective glance upon the hospitable land we were quitting, were speedily wafted to the shores of our native France. At length, the tower of the church of our village rose upon our view, and we quickly afterwards found ourselves there. My brother had gone on before: but joyless was the entrance into our formerly pleasant home: it was quiet, empty, and deserted. No yard-dog greeted us with loud baying; no domestic fowl were chirping about. All had been taken away; and amongst the rest, a little pet of my own, a tame kid, which I had left behind, and the loss of which was to me matter of serious grief. The few things we had brought with us relieved us, at first, from a good deal of embarrassment.

My father felt extremely gratified when, after a few days' interval, one of his old acquaintances paid us a visit, and, calling him aside, put into his hands a purse containing fifty louis d'or, with these words:—"Here, my friend! take it not ill that I have retained your property so long; but I would not give it you until I was convinced that you were in a situation to keep it when you had it."

My father was at a loss to understand this seeming enigma, since this man had been one of the most furious of the self-called patriots, at the period of his imprisonment. "Friend," returned he hesitatingly, "I know not what I should think of you."

"Think what you please," replied the other, "but I will afford you a clew to this riddle. I detested from my soul the horrors which were enacted here and elsewhere; but what could I do? I called to mind the old proverb—'One swallow makes no summer.' I assumed the deportment of a 'good patriot,' because in that character, and in that alone, I should have it in my power essentially to benefit my friends. When I heard that informations were laid against you, I was accordingly among the first who broke into your house, and commenced the work of spoliation; and from my knowledge of the premises, I lost no time in reaching the place where your cash was deposited. This I seized on, and have kept un-appropriated until now, when the return of security enables me to perceive that I may redeliver it to you with safety. I pray you let this secret remain un-violated between us."

My father was unable to utter a word in reply to this explanation; but he pressed his friend's hand, and his grateful countenance spoke the swelling feelings of his heart. This was a great help to us. Fifty louis d'or was, at that time, an important sum, as the republic paid with assignats, and one louis d'or would often fetch the value of a hundred francs in the paper currency. Cattle were now purchased, together with the instruments necessary in our trade; and the house, after the lapse of four weeks, became as cheerful and commodious as if we had never left it.

The French armies passed the Rhine, and victory almost uniformly crowned their banners. The theatre of war was, at several periods, in our immediate neighbourhood; but our little town, somehow or other, always escaped the ravages of plunder. We were, however, occasionally harassed by contributions. The Austrian troops were no strangers to us; but they did not come in sufficient force to do essential injury. My eldest brother was drawn by the conscription: and his lot obliged him to march directly.[2] His regiment was the sixth of cuirassiers, and he made his first campaign in Switzerland. My parents were rendered disconsolate by this bereavement, since the young man was not only an affectionate son, but an intelligent and an active citizen. They were however compelled to seek consolation in the thought that their own case, far from being a solitary one, was shared by many other weeping families.

Meanwhile, the young soldier, having completed his Swiss expedition, was sent into Italy: his regiment was concerned in the battle of Marengo, where General Desaix closed a life of heroism by a death of glory—It subsequently entered Germany, and took part in the battle of Austerlitz. For his good conduct and bravery in this action, my brother was invested with the cross of honour; but he had, to counterbalance this fortune, the ill fate to lose his left leg, which was dashed to pieces by a spent ball. This disabled him from further service, and a pension was settled on him. He therefore returned to us, cured, indeed, but crippled, yet without having been deprived of his natural gaiety of heart and disposition to activity. He procured a wooden leg, which was made with so much dexterity as to hide the deform-

---

2. The laws of the conscription ordained those included within their operation to draw lots, according to which, the time was fixed for their entering upon service, as well as their peculiar destination.

ity consequent upon his loss; and if the substitution was at times perceived, it showed that his cross of honour was not bestowed unworthily. In spite of it, he married a very pretty girl, with a considerable fortune, and was thereby enabled to carry on the business to which he had been bred by his father; and he is now living, I am happy to say, in respectability and comfort.

In the year 1806, I also was included in the conscription list. In this circumstance there was nothing extraordinary, and yet it operated on me like a thunder-stroke: I said nothing of this feeling to my brother; for he was devoted with enthusiasm to the military profession, of which he spoke in terms almost of inspiration.

"Every young man," said he, "who is healthy, and possessed of sufficient strength to bear the inconveniences of the service, ought to repair with ardour to the standard of his country, whenever that country is threatened with danger. I know of no calling so honourable as that of a soldier, who endures, for a slight remuneration, all the privations and horrors of war;— who, reckless of danger, every day exposes his own life for the preservation of his kindred and fellow citizens from the invading enemy. If he falls, he dies the death of glory. Does he become mutilated?—He leaves the scene of his honourable exploits, and carries home with him the esteem of his comrades, receiving there the welcome of affection and respect."

Such were the impassioned observations frequently reiterated by my warlike brother; and I would not have advised any one to thwart him when in this excited state. I had always cherished the hope of drawing a free lot, which would have exempted me from service. This hope was now at an end. I drew the number nine, by virtue of which, I, like my brother before me, was compelled to march without delay. My mother was inconsolable; but my father's sensibility had been blunted by renewed accessions of evil, and he now shielded himself with the feeling of indifference. My brother encouraged me; and when I cast my eye on the red riband of the cross of honour which decorated his button-hole, a spark of emulation darted athwart my mind, and I felt excited to acquire a similar mark of distinction; an ardour however which was speedily abated on glancing a little lower down upon his wooden leg.

Provided with whatever assistance my parents had it in their power to extend to me, I quitted the town with my companions, and an old Sergeant escorted us to the place of our destination, where I was enrolled in a regiment of infantry, the depôt of which was at that period in Strasburg; and consequently I remained some time in the vicinity of my friends. Here my initiation in the art of war took place. Superannuated warriors, themselves past the capability of military service, were our teachers; and these men were the most fitting of any to provide the regiment, from time to time, with efficient recruits. In the beginning of my career, I imbibed a powerful aversion to the duties I was subjected to; nor was this without reason; since, during my former residence in Germany, I had frequent opportunities of witnessing military exercises, and recollected perfectly well the brutal treatment experienced by the unfortunate novices at the hand of their task-masters. It was not enough that a recruit was pushed about and insulted: actual chastisement was inflicted without remorse; and my compassion was constantly awakened by the sufferings of these poor people, whose only offence was awkwardness in performing evolutions entirely new to them. But I soon found, to my inexpressible delight, that this system was not followed up by my instructors, who exercised towards their pupils great kindness and forbearance. Their manner of speaking was considerate, nay affectionate, as should be that of every one who proposes to give instruction to others. Accordingly, we returned their kindness with confidence and respect; using all possible endeavours to comprehend and perform our duties, in order to relieve them, as much as possible, from the trouble necessarily entailed on them.

During the whole time of my stay at Strasburg, my friends at home were in the habit of furnishing me with articles of comfort and convenience; and thus my residence there was, all things considered, agreeable enough. In the evenings, when we had assembled together, the veterans related to us their former expeditions and achievements—not in the spirit of boasting, or to impress upon our minds the hardships of a military life; but in order to lay before their youthful auditors an example of the manner in which they ought to behave themselves when called on for active service. Thus the days passed cheerfully on; and a positive desire was awakened in our hearts to join the ranks of our regiment, in order that we might display to our aged friends how much we had profited by their lessons.

The French armies were, at the period of which I speak, in Suabia, Bavaria, and Franconia,[3] ready to commence on the instant a projected expedition against Prussia; and our men were eager to receive orders to march thither. But affairs took another turn. The expedition was undertaken and completed without our intervention. Its result was fortunate for France; and our disappointment was great in being doomed to remain inactive in quarters while these glorious events were going forward.

So passed the autumn of 1806. The succeeding year brought

---

3. The provinces of Suabia and Franconia appertain to the former division of Germany, when it constituted an empire collectively, and was separated into districts, or circles, (kreise) at the head of each of which was a duke, or other potentate, not possessing, however, supreme sovereignty, but subordinate to the emperor, who was nominally an elected monarch, and in whom was vested absolute dominion over this vast and beautiful country. The imperial title and power had long been engrossed by the house of Lorraine (archdukes of Austria), at the period when Napoleon Buonaparte, then Emperor of the French, annulled this order of things. In the year 1800 the empire of Germany was dissolved, and broken up into various independent states;—the different petty princes, some of them remaining dukes, and others elevated to the title of kings,—for instance, the kings of Saxony, Wirtemberg, Bavaria, etc.—but each exercising sovereign power. The circle of Suabia, accordingly, is now transformed into the kingdom of Wirtemberg, whilst that of Franconia is merged in the kingdom of Bavaria. It is, in fact, a matter of great difficulty for any, except those who are either natives of Germany, or have travelled a good deal therein, to acquire clear ideas respecting its political geography. It is, at present, divided into thirty-three independent states, greater or lesser in point of wealth and general consequence; the independence, however, I am sorry to add, resides not in the people, but wholly in their governments, even there where a so-called Constitution has been dispensed, as a favour rather than a right, by the sovereign to his subjects.

with it fresh occurrences. Spain called in France as a confederate against England, and the prudent Napoleon made use of this circumstance to further his own peculiar views. For a long while there was a report circulated that we should take part in an expedition to Spain; but it was only a report: the summer passed away, and we were still at Strasburg.

Suddenly an order arrived for breaking up our quarters, and in three days time we found ourselves on the road to Paris. We formed a battalion of seven hundred men, the conscripts of the present year being united with us. The march to Paris was the pleasantest I ever experienced in the course of my military life. Our daily journeys were short; the landlords and landladies of the inns on the road were courteous and obliging; we had most of us spare money in our pockets; and these advantages, added to the excitement of new scenes, remarkable places, and a beautiful country, combined to render us happy.

We were speedily in Paris; and I can scarcely express the extent of my wonder at the first view of this noble city, both externally and internally. We were conducted almost close to the Tuileries; and having been reviewed there by a commissary of war, were sent to occupy an empty barrack in the suburb of St. Germain. Everything had been provided for our reception. Our stay here was protracted for some days, it being the custom at that time for every detachment of troops to receive a festive dinner before their departure to join the army.

The tables were spread in a public place, to enable all the men of the battalion to enjoy themselves in concert. A number of toasts were drunk, which was the occasion of a great deal of amusement; and many comic scenes ensued. After the dinner, I went to look round Paris; and was equally astonished and delighted at the variety and splendour of the scenes around me, and at the spirit of life and bustle which seemed to animate the population of the metropolis, thronging in every direction. Coaches were rattling about on all sides; and groups of gay horsemen occasionally diversified the scene. When the time arrived for my return to my quarters, I was obliged to take some trouble in seeking them out; and the same difficulty, I found, had occurred to several of my companions. Every one of us retired to rest, full of gratification and of amazement at the novelties we had witnessed; and the next morning we quitted Paris.

We were now certain that Spain was our destination. Many regiments left the metropolis at the same period, with a similar object. Our route lay through Orleans, where I saw the statue of Jeanne D'Arc, her helm and shield by her side, which is placed in a public part of the town, enclosed by a palisading. This sight called up the memory of past times into my mind, and gave occasion for instituting a comparison between those and the present.

We quitted Orleans, proceeded to Limoges, thence into the rich town of Bordeaux, and subsequently to Paul de Dax, remarkable for its hot springs. From this place we proceeded to Bayonne, where all appeared full of military activity, as it was the general rendezvous of the troops destined for the Spanish expedition. The whole army consisted of young conscripts, principally of the current year: not a beard was visible upon the chins of the incipient heroes; and hence we were facetiously denominated L'Armée des Enfans. Many—many a one of these youths, then full of hope and strength, was doomed to see his native France no more: many were starved in the Peninsula; and no account having been rendered of them, are perhaps still expected at home—alas! in vain.

CHAPTER 2

To Spain with Dupont

The Grand Duke of Berg (Murat) was General-in-Chief of the army of Spain. As soon as he arrived with his staff, orders were given to advance. At the close of the year 1807, we set foot for the first time on Spanish ground. We belonged to the second division of the army, commanded by Gen. Dupont. Another division proceeded, through Spain, into Portugal, to occupy and defend it against the English. Although the provisions for the soldiery were none of the best in France, in Spain they were far worse. In the former country every one received the means to furnish his journey with necessary comforts, including a good bed, with blankets and mattresses. However, a soldier should not accustom himself to expect such accommodations; and our first night's lodging in Spain was calculated to put our philosophy to the proof. About four o'clock in the afternoon, Bayonne was behind us; and an hour afterwards night set in. We procured for ourselves flambeaux, which are commonly to be met with; and our column exhibited a regular train of torch-bearers. The march was extremely tedious and inconvenient, from the irregularity of the road: but, in spite of all impediments, we on the same night effected the passage of the Bidassoa, a little river which separates Spain from France. How different were the manners of the inhabitants on either side of this river! Angry and malicious glances were abundantly cast on us by the Spaniards.

A little further on, we came to a small village, at which we halted for the night, the cavalry proceeding a league further, to a somewhat larger place. We received billets for our night's lodging, but they were of no use whatever, since we saw none of the inhabitants, who kept themselves out of the way from want either of courtesy or confidence. At length some of these people were reluctantly dragged forward, and compelled to give the troops both information and assistance. I was fortunate enough, with two of my comrades, to find a comfortable lodging—at least what would be so called in Spain. Our landlord was a wealthy inhabitant of the village, who treated us with the utmost hospitality a Spaniard is capable of showing. Our party consisted of a German, a Spaniard, and two Frenchmen. Each man spoke only his native tongue, and hence our conversation was of the most droll and ridiculous character; since, urged by the social principle, every one was anxious to communicate to his neighbour his own wants and observations; and having discovered that this could not be effected by words, looks, signs, and gestures were resorted to, often of the most grotesque description,—sometimes understood, sometimes not, and almost always giving rise to violent bursts of laughter. Altogether, it was a highly comic scene. Our supper consisted of various Spanish dishes, by no means wanting in oil and pepper,—ingredients used here in an abundance which did not well agree with our taste. But the landlord tempered his repast with a bottle of good Spanish wine, to which we had not the slightest objection. Our bed was of straw, to which our cloaks, &c. formed the blankets and sheets; but our night's rest was dreadfully disturbed by a violent draught of wind; although excessive fatigue made even this uncomfortable dwelling acceptable.

We awoke the next morning with but a slight sense of refreshment, and our limbs were benumbed with cold. We took leave of our landlord, and repaired to the place of rendezvous. Here we were literally stunned by the exclamations and complaints made by our comrades of the manner in which they had passed the night. From this time we no longer received marching money, in lieu of which rations were substituted, consisting of the usual portion of bread, half a pound of meat, and half a pint of wine. Having arrived at the village already mentioned late in the evening, these rations were not distributed until the following morning before we commenced our march. The wine we drank immediately, not indeed as a matter of choice, but owing to the fact of our being destitute of vessels to carry it in. The meat was cut in pieces and stowed into our knapsacks, and the vegetables which accompanied it we gave to the poorer inhabitants of the place. Thus provided, we renewed our march. The road by which we travelled overlooked a country of great beauty, leading us alternately over high mountains and through deep valleys. We were met by a great number of Biscayan carts, the motion of which produced a sound excessively disagreeable to our ears, owing to their wheels not turning round the axis, but with it, and thence occasioning a grinding and rumbling that jarred to the very centre of our auricular organs. These carts are used throughout the whole district of the Pyrenees, being calculated to make way across the very worst roads.

Our second night's lodging in Spain was at the town of Tolosa. There we were not permitted to mix with the inhabitants, but were accommodated in a convent, which had been converted for our reception into barracks. We found plenty of straw wherewith to make us beds—not the most luxurious mode of recumbency, but by no means to be despised by the followers of martial glory. Rations were served out to us this evening of the same proportion and quality as in the morning; and in the course of an hour, all our kettles were put in requisition to boil the meat. We had pease for vegetables; but so craving was our appetite, that neither vegetables nor meat were sufficiently dressed. Hunger was in this instance the best cook, and imparted to our humble fare a relish which more costly viands, without it, would have been destitute of. It was really pleasant to observe the manner in which ten or twelve men would congregate round a kettle of soup, each armed with his spoon, and all attacking it at the same moment. Hilarity and good-humour prevailed: as our appetite subsided, we found leisure to concoct and pass round the joke or jibe, careless as to the novelty or refinement of our pleasantry, and contented to enjoy the mirth that was cheaply provided. Supper over, we nestled in our straw, and experienced a far more comfortable slumber than that which attended us the former night.

Such was the nature of our daily march. We slept, by turns, in a church or a convent. The strictest discipline was enforced, and the least breach thereof visited with a heavy punishment. The abundant rains which now marked the approach of the wet season deluged the otherwise fine roads with water and mud, and rendered them most inconvenient and slippery; the small mountain rivulets which we had to cross were swollen into considerable streams; and many a night we found ourselves without the means to dry our drenched garments.

We arrived successively at Mondragon, and Salines; and finally halted at Vittoria, where we were joined by the troops which followed in our route.

The object of our expedition into Spain was now made generally known. The French army was destined, in unison with the Spanish troops, to oppose the operations of the English. This at least was the understanding then prevalent; but the course of events proved how far our government had miscalculated the sentiments of the people of the Peninsula.

Our army consisted of 80,000 men; and after having been reviewed by Murat, proceeded into the interior of the country. Even already it became sufficiently apparent that the natives cherished a violent hatred for their auxiliaries; insomuch that, in many places, we perceived marks of an outburst of the smouldering fire. This spirit was however, in the beginning, always put down by the strong arm of power, and hence the indignation and distrust of the Spaniards increased twofold.

We were now in full march towards Madrid; and our movements were hastened in consequence of information that several popular commotions had begun to show themselves in that metropolis, instigated by the conduct of Don Manuel Godoy, the Prince of the Peace. Murat, at our head, led us onward through Miranda, a town on the Ebro, and through Burgos, until the walls of Madrid rose upon our view.

The season was extremely unfavourable, the rain falling in torrents. In spite of this, however, we were compelled to remain three days in tents, without the city. I know not what, motives influenced the authorities to this course; but at the termination of the three days, the whole of the magistrates came in a body, with the corregidor at their head, and presented to our general-in-chief the keys of the town. Shortly after, we entered the capital, with flying colours and resonant music; but scarcely any of the inhabitants greeted our arrival, and those who did lounge about to stare upon us as we passed consisted of the lowest rabble. The fine appearance and consummate discipline of the French troops appeared to excite a feeling of admiration, but not one friendly look or exclamation of welcome was extended towards our lines. Individuals of the higher classes occasionally exhibited themselves at the balconies; and their dark faces and lowering brows were in perfect harmony with the expression of their humbler fellow-citizens. We saw no women whatever, the custom of the country not permitting their free intercourse with men even of their own nation; and it therefore not being to be wondered at that they were sedulously kept out of our sight.[1]

Our troops were, in the first instance, quartered partly in empty

1. A German gentleman, who was sojourning in Madrid at this eventful period, wrote an account to a friend of the reception of the French troops under Murat. He gives, however, a very different report of the circumstances attending this reception from that published in the French Moniteur; stating the hostile feeling of the Spaniards to have been, by no means, confined to the frowning looks and suspicions spoken of by our friend, the author of this little volume; but on the contrary, manifested, even then, by acts of the most unequivocal violence—by the discharge of whole volleys of stones—by the emptying of vessels filled with boiling water out of the windows—by the distribution of poisoned victuals—and by assassination. In fact, that precious political journal, the Moniteur, was never worthy of the slightest particle of credit, since it was avowedly used by the emperor as an engine for forcing any description of facts he chose upon the belief of his good citizens o Paris. After all, when we reflect on the present government of Spain, and on the mockery of a king who sways its sceptre, it is a pity that the Spanish people made any opposition whatever to the establishment of a new dynasty; or rather, that they did not fight with the same enthusiasm for Napoleon and Joseph, as they did, for so long a series of years, against them.

barracks, and partly in convents, the cloisters of which latter were prepared for their reception, and provided with beds. Meanwhile the king and queen departed from Madrid to Bayonne, whither the Prince of Asturias had preceded them, in order to hold the celebrated conference with Napoleon. This step was very contrary to the wishes and opinions of the people; but, like the generality of crowned heads, that of Charles IV. was self-willed and impotent, and he went. This proceeding tended more and more to irritate the minds and tempers of the Spaniards; and the disturbances which had from the beginning been habitual between them and ourselves wore every day a more serious aspect. In the public houses, more especially, where the effects of wine aggravated the national jealousy, bad words were constantly followed up by hard blows, and blood flowed profusely, gushing out at the stroke of the poniard or at the push of the bayonet. Our officers did all that lay in their power to prevent the recurrence of these scenes: but their efforts were vain; and instead of decreasing, they grew more and more frequent, the name of Spaniard becoming synonymous with hatred to France and Frenchmen. Assassination by night and insult by day were the agreeable constituents of our life in Madrid; and hence perpetual watchfulness, particularly when the shades of night fell over us, was necessary for the preservation of our very existence. Nor was this spirit confined to the metropolis: on the contrary, every provincial district displayed equal urbanity towards us, and revelled in similar scenes. The genius of revolution was, in truth, busy here, there, everywhere around; and a moral convulsion of the most appalling kind threatened to engulf us in its destructive consequences.

On the 27th of April, in the city of Toledo, all restraint was thrown aside, and the flame of discord fairly broke out; in order to extinguish which, our battalion, together with some others, was dispatched thither. But before I proceed with this part of my narrative, I will give the reader as good an idea as close observation enabled me to form, of the Spanish character.

The Spaniard is proud, and thinks himself privileged to regard with supreme contempt the native of any other country: he is extremely vindictive; and having resolved to sacrifice any individual to his revenge, it is with great difficulty his victim can escape. He will treasure up his venom from year to year; and when a more generous spirit would imagine the sense of injury had been wholly blunted, will spring, tiger like, upon his prey. He is, in the highest degree, jealous, luxurious, voluptuous; in a word, whatever vices disfigure the human breast are to be found nowhere so rife as in the bosom of a Spaniard.[2] Degradingly superstitious, he receives for gospel whatever the knavish monks choose to assert, without daring even to question its veracity. Miracles are with him matters of common-place notoriety; and every church is filled with pictures of saints, who are reported to be very liberal of their intervention.—There is however some brightness on the reverse of the medal. The Spaniard possesses the virtues of sobriety and fortitude. The greatest inconveniences are borne by him with a degree of patience truly admirable; and love of his native land becomes in his breast a sacred principle; as was sufficiently manifested in the long peninsular struggle against Napoleon.[3]

Our route to Toledo led us through Aranjuez, where the splendid summer palace of the king is situated, in a country perfectly enchanting, and ten leagues from Madrid. Hence we

---

2. The English reader will bear in mind, that it is probable a sense of injury jaundiced the perceptions of the French soldier who wrote this account; nevertheless, in sober sadness, we fear his allegations are in many instances but too well founded.

3. This description of the Spanish character bears, as we have already observed in the margin, the stamp of a little partiality or prejudice. I need only suggest to my readers the former greatness of the population of this beautiful country to impress upon their minds a high sense, not only of its capabilities, but of what it has actually accomplished. in the time of the Moorish dominion there, Spain was the very region of romance and poetry; and a glance at the discovery by Cortes of the hitherto unknown continent of America will suffice to render it equally celebrated for the spirit of noble enterprise. Who so gallant, who so high-minded, in the field of chivalry, as the Spanish cavalier? The idea of being thought capable of an unworthy act would have caused his own eloquent blood to rush into his cheeks, and that of his whole host of forefathers into his recollection. In works of art and literature, likewise, they occupied a proud station, as evidently appears from their splendid palaces and Gothic structures; from the pencil of Velasquez and Murillo, and from the pen of Cervantes.

proceeded to Ocanias, and from that place onwards to the scene of revolt. When we arrived at Toledo, the greatest exertion was necessary to quell the insurrection. The Spaniards had armed themselves, and were running in agitation through all the streets of the town; the monks were preaching rebellion; and anarchy reigned throughout the whole city. Several discharges of musketry were levelled by us at the insurgents, and many of them were killed or wounded. This instilled into their minds a sentiment of fear, and produced that kind of quiet which is the result of compulsion, and only prognosticates further evil,—like the brief suspension of the tempest, while the rack on high is gathering materials for a fresh out-bursting. Before our arrival, the houses of the more peaceable citizens had been broken open, and thoroughly sacked; such of their inhabitants as either could not or would not seek safety in flight were poniarded. Here, for the first time, I grew fully acquainted with the feeling experienced by a soldier when in presence of his enemy; and although the action was not of long duration, several of our men received awkward wounds. We stopped at Toledo for some days, during which period we were pretty comfortably accommodated; and then, leaving a strong- garrison behind us, returned to Madrid.

The greatest portion of the French army had for some time occupied an encampment round about the capital, and a feeble garrison only remained withinside the walls, scarcely sufficient, indeed, to occupy the most important stations. The Spaniards availed themselves of this circumstance to hatch a conspiracy, the object of which was to take the French unawares, and massacre them by wholesale. It was easy to observe that, for a few days past, the population of Madrid had been receiving a considerable re-inforcement. A great number of peasants poured into the capital from the adjacent country districts: nevertheless our suspicions were not aroused; and such was the aspect of affairs when the sun uprose on the morning of the fatal second of May.

Certain members of the Spanish royal family had projected repairing to France under an escort of our troops. Against this measure, the faces of the people were steadily set; and on the day above mentioned, a furious mob overthrew the sentinels at the royal palace, entered its walls, and poniarded sundry French officers, who were so unfortunate as to fall in their way. This was the signal for universal revolt. The cry "to arms!" resounded through the streets, which were paraded by bands of insurgents, who slew every Frenchman they met. The guards were overpowered, and the residences of several general officers despoiled of every article of value therein. Our little garrison made a most courageous resistance: but what heroism can protract a contest against numbers? They fell covered with wounds and with honour; and meanwhile the host of rebels was hourly accumulating.

At length reinforcements arrived from the encampment; and this event soon changed the course of circumstances. The French troops advanced with great celerity. They took no heed of the missiles aimed at them from the balconies; but bore right forward to the assistance and rescue of their overwhelmed comrades. Possessed by a feeling of indignation and rage, they hesitated not to retaliate upon the misguided natives, who in their turn were either shot or struck to the earth, and were very speedily undeceived as to their comparative strength. They fled in all directions; but were every where encountered by fresh detachments of hostile troops.

Is it to be wondered at, that, assailed by treachery and assassination, these men forgot for awhile the sacred emotions of compassion?—They saw nothing but the mangled bodies of their fellow-countrymen; they heard nothing but their agonising shrieks for quarter or for help.—They took deadly vengeance, sparing neither age nor profession. The sanctuary of the churches was invaded, and the penitent at the altar shared the fate of the armed rebel. The sacred stole of the priest was no greater protection from the soldier's mad vengeance, than the sober garb of the citizen. The vestments and plate applied to the uses of religion were abstracted without remorse, and the unhallowed appetite of lust was let loose upon the persons both of matrons and virgins. It is with grief I speak it, but truth compels me to admit that every conceivable atrocity marked the vengeance of the French soldiery.

A portion of the insurgents had occupied the arsenal, and taken possession of the arms accumulated there; but their further measures were arrested by the arrival of a French detachment, and themselves put to the sword, a few only escaping by flight. Even the unhappy individuals consigned by sickness to the wards of the hospitals were thrown out of bed and inhumanly lacerated—until, the first ebullitions of rage having subsided, other detachments of troops interposed, and put a stop to the scene of carnage.

As the day advanced, the French forces continued to arrive in still increasing numbers. The cavalry scoured the principal streets, overthrowing every thing that presented itself; the infantry pursued a similar course in the lesser ones; and the point of the bayonet pierced alike children of ten or twelve years, and persons who had arrived at manhood. One of our grenadiers encountered a young woman of high respectability, who, while she held a child on one arm, brandished a poniard with the other hand: he stunned the mother by a blow with the butt-end of his musket, and impaled her infant upon his bayonet. In another place, a Mameluke rode up full gallop, each hand filled with watches, which he held by their chains: "Camerade, en voulez-vous une?"—He was answered by each of those who were near him taking one; and thus a very beautiful gold watch fell to my share.

Instances similar to the above were common enough. When the Spaniards perceived that their case was desperate, they gave in, and promised submission. But we knew that the seeds of hatred were too deeply sown to produce other than the deadliest fruit; and placing no confidence in their forced subserviency, we stood upon our guard. The sentinels were everywhere doubled; and a piquet of 1500 men was in daily motion. Thus the inhabitants of Madrid were kept quiet; but in the neighbouring country, armed forces were constantly assembling: General Caro was put at the head of these, in the province of Valencia: in Andalusia, Generals Reding and Castanos took the command. Marshal Moncey was dispatched against the Valencian rebels; and General Dupont against the Andalusian.—And now commences the history of my sufferings.

CHAPTER 3

War in Andalusia

On the last day of May, 1808, the corps of General Dupont quitted Madrid, on its march to Andalusia. It consisted of about 17,000 men capable of bearing arms. Our daily orders forbade, under strict penalties, any wrong to be offered to the inhabitants of the country; and General Dupont was uniformly a man of his word. The weather was fine; the distance short; the provision for the troops pretty good: for the most part, however, we were under the necessity of bivouacking at night, and thus came but slightly in contact with the natives. We went through the province of La Mancha; crossed, without any difficulty whatever, the gloomy valleys of the Sierra Morena, and arrived at Andujar, where the army for the first time halted in order to concentrate itself. Notice quickly reached us, that several parties of the enemy had collected in front, for the purpose of intercepting our march; and on the 7th of June we attacked these troops by Alcolea: after some hours' resistance, they were dispersed, and two pieces of cannon fell into our hands.

Another day, when on our road to Cordova, we met with some of our comrades, who had been the preceding day taken prisoners by the Spaniards. But what, an appearance did they present! Their eyes were put out; their tongues cut off; their fingers split up; and sundry parts of their body stabbed. Everyone who saw them was filled with horror at so appalling a spectacle, and swore to revenge a hundredfold the barbarity with which they had been treated. Quite different had been the usage of the

Spanish captives by us: they were provided for well, and sent to their respective homes, the greater part of them being country people, who resided near at hand. At length we reached Cordova. The gates of the town were closed, and we were received with discharges of cannon and musketry. Every peaceful proposition was rejected, and even the bearers of them insulted. The patience of our commander at last gave way, and he ordered a general attack: a battery of twelve-pounders was erected, and a breach made. The sappers, their advance covered by a troop of upwards of a hundred soldiers, burst open the gates, and our forces immediately rushed into the town like the impetuous waves of ocean. Our antagonists consisted of about two thousand regular troops, amongst whom were a good many Germans; but their resistance was weak and inefficient, opposed to French warriors who were urged forward by rage, without fear either of death or bonds. When in the town, our men dispersed, and in small groups ran along the streets overthrowing both citizens and soldiers; and every where round arose the shouts of the conquerors and the cry of the dying victims. Every house was forced open; and all who presented themselves drew down instant destruction. The temples of worship were robbed, and profaned in different ways; and the utmost ingenuity exhibited in varying the insults and tortures inflicted upon the unhappy townsfolk. Neither childhood nor old age proved an exception from the; prevailing thirst for blood. In short, all feelings of humanity had fled.

The town of Jaen shared the same fate, its resistance having been similar. Our soldiers were literally burdened with spoils of gold and silver. The treasures of Cordova and of its churches were in our knapsacks, and many a costly crucifix peeped from beneath their covers, the purloiner not having had time to secure it more completely.

By this conduct, it may be easily imagined that the angry passions of the Spaniards grew more and more inflamed, and only awaited opportunity to retaliate. No one attached to the French army dared venture beyond the circle of his companions without the consciousness of exposing himself to a death of horrible torture. It is true, that every Spaniard accused of ill-treating a Frenchman was subjected to the severest punishment—exceeding, if possible, his own barbarity: yet, in spite of these examples, their savage vengeance was constantly renewed. Their watchword [1] was *Vencer o morir por nuestra patria.*[2]

So long as the season remained favourable, this kind of life, however unpleasant, might be tolerated. We had lost a great many men in various ways; in open battle, by assassination, by sickness, arising from the Spanish climate, where after the hottest summer day, the dews of night fall heavy and cold, proving a great discomfort to us, who were as yet not inured to the privations and sufferings of war. Indeed the most robust men, whilst unused to it, are incapable of bearing the Spanish climate without annoyance.

The entire province of Andalusia took up arms. The monks upraised the war-cry from the pulpits of peace. Every slain Frenchman was a source of profit to the individual who slew him, and the deed was held to entitle him to heavenly as well as to earthly rewards. Thus our situation became daily more hazardous. We quitted Cordova, and fell back on Andujar, before General Castanos, whose army, doubling ours in number, was in full march against us, whilst another not inconsiderable force was manoeuvring to cut off our retreat. We found no difficulty, however, in dispersing this latter armament.

On the 14th of July, General Reding attacked us with an army of 18,000 troops of the line, and a strong artillery. The bat-

---

1. This patriotic watch-word recalls to our memory the brave Lacedemonians, who left their homes,—each man enthusiastic in his resolution to preserve the liberty of his country, and either to return victorious or to perish gloriously. It is but justice to a fallen people to bear in mind that no land has presented, in this respect, a greater resemblance to ancient Greece than Spain. The Greek wars of liberty have been renewed in that devoted country, from time to time, from the commencement of their history even until the present era; and it may perhaps, after all, not be too much to assert, that if ever the continental nations of Europe obtain political freedom, the example will be even yet set to them by Spain.
2. Let us conquer or die for our country.

tle was obstinate on both sides, and I saw numbers of my comrades falling around me. Our powder was quickly exhausted, and a fresh supply distributed, on the receipt of which we advanced, raising the much loved cry of "Vive l'Empereur!" Night put a stop to the action; and the Spaniards retreated in good order to their old position.

Next morning the battle was renewed. We fought with equal bravery as on the preceding day: every inch of ground was disputed; and the shades of evening again fell upon the earth whilst we were pursuing our sanguinary toil.

On the third day, the 16th of July, the enemy, in order to decide the victory, brought up his whole power; but their best endeavours were rendered unavailing by the good conduct of our troops. The Spanish forces had suffered severely; and we also missed a great proportion of our brave fellows, to whom the inhospitable ground yielded a bloody grave. Numbers were wounded; and the situation of these unfortunate men was cruelly wretched. Destitute of careful treatment, their hurts scarcely dressed, they found hardly any shelter from the intolerable heat of the sun; and in this condition a good many were literally starved, who with average care might have been preserved to do service to their country, and honour to their friends. But misery and want are inseparably linked to the chariot of war: men, it is true, grow accustomed even to these evils; and seldom does the soldier look with tenderness upon the sufferings of his comrade, heedless that the following hour may bring to himself a similar fate.

When the Spaniards perceived that all their efforts fell short of the mark, they desisted from further violence, and the general state of the country became more tranquil. This quiet however was to us but temporary; for after awhile appeared another foe, of a character far more formidable, and a contention with whom was likely to be attended with still greater horrors. Whilst the fruits of the earth continued tolerably plentiful, its produce rendered us elate, and restrained all disposition to repining: but when our protracted sojourn, added to the ravages of war and the licenses of excess, had exhausted the kindly supplies of nature, then approached the grim fiend hunger. Many a day did we pass without receiving a morsel of bread, being restricted to a small portion of meat accompanied with wretched soup; and at length, even this provision likewise ceased, and we were compelled to resort to whatever substitutes fell in our way, among which maybe enumerated the herbs which grew uncultivated in the open fields. By this kind of living, every description of malady was successively introduced amongst us, and a necessity arose for sundry medicines, with which we were wholly unprovided, our field-dispensaries having fallen into the hands of the Spaniards during our passage through the Sierra Morena. From these causes, our army decreased rapidly; yet, in spite of all, and in the midst of every other deprivation, we were not abandoned by the principle of courage; much of our fortitude being doubtless owing to the circumstance of each man suffering not solitarily, but in common with his companions.

Our brigade, commanded by General Wedel, was ordered to march to La Carolina; and in the mean time, General Dupont was again engaged in battle with General Reding, upon whose army he made several desperate attacks; but the Spanish chieftain would not yield, and eventually Dupont found himself so situated as to be induced to capitulate. Of these events, General Wedel had no knowledge at the time of their occurrence: he therefore descended from the mountains upon a Spanish corps, which he attacked, making prisoners of a whole regiment, together with two pieces of cannon: but not being in sufficient force to protract the combat, we fell back into our strong holds, and were there encountered by another division of the enemy; and thus unequally opposed, we also had no alternative but to lay down our arms.

The French forces thus compelled to surrender, consisted of 14,000 men, 3,000 having been previously killed or wounded. Our situation had become so exceedingly irksome, that this capitulation seemed likely to improve our prospects rather than the contrary. The terms of it were, to disarm ourselves, and then to be sent back to France: but let us see how this latter stipulation was observed.

No sooner had we grounded our arms, than the Spaniards broke in on us, and murdered in cold blood our defenceless people. The hostile generals, it is true, interposed, and used every possible means to quell this diabolical spirit, but in vain. The ill-starred men who thus fell victims to treachery met death under every variety of torture: some were pierced with numberless stabs; others taken and burnt alive; in short, all the horrors of Cordova were revived, and put in execution against us.

When glutted with carnage, they took breathing time, and the remainder of our hapless troops were left to indulge the melancholy anticipation of a similar fate. The day passed by, and no food was distributed to us; so that we began to suppose starvation was the doom for which we were reserved. The keen pangs of hunger overcame, in us, even the horror of our brutal oppressors, and we implored them, in piteous accents, to give us wherewithal to eat; but our petitions only awakened their derision. Several men fell down from exhaustion; and these were at once dispatched either with the bayonet, or by a deadly blow from the butt-end of the musket. We were finally conducted back to Cordova, which we had before entered in the character of proud victors; and scarcely could a more woebegone and withering spectacle be presented than that offered by our ranks.

On our arrival in the city, more sufferings awaited our forlorn bands. The infuriated populace rushed upon us like tigers, and individuals were here and there plucked from the line, and literally cut into pieces. Our escort opposed but little resistance to this lawless spirit: they for the most part entrenched themselves in stony-hearted apathy; and even had it been otherwise, they did not possess sufficient strength to preserve our security, invaded as it was by persons of all ranks and all ages. The agonizing throes and convulsive gestures of expiring nature were gazed on with savage exultation, and human charity appeared to have given place to the devilish temper of the cannibal. Even one of their own countrymen, a soldier in the ranks of our escort, was struck down in my sight because he had wrapped himself in a French coat, being destitute of any other. His comrades interfered, but to no purpose: the man was mercilessly butchered.

No time was now lost in conveying us to various places of strength; but these were immediately surrounded by our blood-thirsty enemies, and nothing but the solid walls, and a newly-awakened vigilance on the part of our escort, saved our exhausted remnant.

Happy were we—comparatively happy—when we found ourselves out of this detested town. Our columns were severally dispatched along different roads; and in each direction were we met by armed bands, and saw the natives undergoing military exercises; whilst the dreadful cry of *Matomos los Franceses!*[3] rung in our ears.

It had been promised that we should embark at Barameda de San Lucar, in order to reach our native France; and the prospect of shortly escaping out of this land of slaughter animated our minds with a sort of fearful hope. Before this longed-for period occurred, however, new sufferings were in store for us. In proportion as our distance from Cordova increased, the hazard of immediate death grew less and less imminent; but to counterbalance this comfort, we were more and more exposed to the insults of our escort, who renewed their own barbarity as soon as other dangers were removed. They permitted us not to deviate one step out of the line, even to satisfy any pressing want; and in the night we were cooped up in ruinous buildings filled with loathsome vermin, being fed upon bread and water, and this in stinted quantities.

Our numbers thinned rapidly. Fatigue and insufficient provision rendered many incapable of rising to renew their march after the night's halt, and dawn exhibited to us the stiffened limbs of such as death had released from further earthly trouble. The survivors were gaunt and emaciated; and frequently on our ghastly march a poor fellow would drop to earth in the extremity of weariness and despair. No effort was made to assist these sufferers,

---

3. Kill the Frenchmen!

who were either left behind to perish, or bayoneted on the spot. It is impossible to tell how many were thus lost: in fact, it seemed to be the intention of the Spaniards to extirpate us altogether.

At length we arrived at San Lucar. Hope, ever an active principle of the human breast, worked busily in us even yet. We said to each other, "Surely our misery will now find a termination!" but no, our enemies had not filled up the measure of their atrocity. We were thrown some of us into prison-ships, other into stinking casemates.[4] The extremity of anguish by which we were now overwhelmed exceeds all powers of description, but may be imagined by the benevolent mind. With scarce power enough to crawl to our detestable dungeons, many reached them only to lie down and die broken-hearted; nor should these be considered unhappy, since they were taken from the evil to come. My lot was cast in one of these putrid casemates, where poisonous dews constantly distilled from the walls, which excluded effectually the free air and sweet light of heaven. Unwholesome and distasteful bread, accompanied by about four ounces of horse-beans and a little rancid oil, formed the materials of our wretched fare—so wretched, that it was in many instances refused even by men fainting with weariness and famished with hunger. Hence the ravages of disease were spread in every direction amongst us; and it was not until death hovered over the heads of the sufferers that they were removed to the hospitals,—which removal indeed was scarcely a change for the better.

Still hope did not quite forsake us, although it was sadly dashed by the taunts of the townspeople, who frequently visited in order to reproach us. They seemed to regard us actually as monsters, and said that it was vain for us to expect ever to tread again upon French ground, as a large reinforcement of our countrymen were in the act of marching to Madrid, but would be resisted by the brave Spaniards under the command of Castanos, Palafox, and others, who would quickly beat them back again.

---

4. A term used in fortification, and designating a subterraneous or covered arch-work.

46

In spite of these vauntings, however, the French troops a second time found the way to Madrid, penetrated into all the recesses of the Peninsula, and finally occupied the coasts. Of these events we were kept in ignorance: but we could observe, from the nature of the preparations constantly going on, and which we were compelled to take part in, receiving abundant stripes for our recompense, that the boasted superiority of our taskmasters was merely ideal. Our situation was after a while altered, and we were sent to Cadiz, the Spaniards not conceiving San Lucar to be a place of sufficient security. Such among us as were at all able to endure the fatigues of the journey were dispatched on foot, and the remainder on board Spanish vessels. In every town through which the former division passed, we saw military exercises in use, and preparations made for the hostile reception of our countrymen.

Having reached Cadiz, we found our treatment still more oppressive than at the place we had quitted, although we had an opportunity of watching more distinctly the course of events. We were again confined in prison-ships, and liberated galleyslaves were set over us as guards; and it should seem that they had been selected on the principle of infamy and ruffianism, for never did I elsewhere encounter such depraved wretches.

As soon as we had got on board these vessels, we were counted like so many cattle when driven into their stables. Each place of rest was made to contain six men; so that when once laid on our backs, we had no room to enable us to change our position either to the right or left; and, as may be easily conceived, the pestilential effluvia arising from so many bodies thus huddled together was offensive in the extreme, rendering the atmosphere of the ship quite putrid. Vermin were generated by thousands; and such was the climax of wretchedness and disgust which oppressed me, that with fervent sincerity I implored the intervention of the destroying angel. The least offence conceived at our behaviour on the part of our masters occasioned the exercise of unrelenting severity. No slave no brute animal, could receive harder treatment at the hands of his owner than did we, who partook of the same common nature with our oppressors, and were born as free as they. A great many of my harassed companions sought refuge from misery by plunging into the sea; others resorted to a different mode of self-destruction; others again perished under the hands of the medical practitioners, who, fiend-like, are said to have, in several instances, drugged their patients with poisonous instead of healing draughts, thinking perhaps that our hapless comrades presented proper subjects on whom to work experiments. The reader will easily imagine that the various causes which I have mentioned had reduced in a woeful degree the number of those troops who had originally laid down arms; and yet the minister of fate availed himself of additional instruments. Worn out as we were, whilst the principle of life remained, the desire of freedom was co-existent with it; and goaded to desperation, we formed several conspiracies against our tyrants, which were uniformly discovered, and as uniformly punished with death. These victims were brought to the fore-part of the vessel, where, confronting the shadowy king, they met his rude embrace without a murmur.

In one instance, however, fortune smiled upon a party of our fellow-sufferers, who, to the number of thirteen men and some officers, escaped in a boat, eluding the vigilance of their guards. I know not if they were ultimately saved, having from that day to the present never received any intelligence of their fate.

An offer was now made to such of us as yet stubbornly contested with our destiny to enter as recruits into the Spanish army! The advantages of the service were insisted on with great vehemence, in the hopes of thus inveigling from us our consent; but their advances were universally rejected with contempt. Not one man amongst us could be found willing to brand his name with infamy by associating with the murderers of his comrades.

Meanwhile the French forces entered Andalusia, and were reported to be advancing upon Cadiz. We were consequently removed from the prison-ships into smaller vessels, in order to be conveyed to a more distant port, but whither we had not the least idea, since none of us were permitted to come upon deck, on peril of being instantly struck down; the only exceptions to which rule were in favour of those who performed the menial offices indispensably necessary amongst us.

After a voyage of eight days, during which the sailors were constantly offering up prayers for fair weather and favourable winds to the Holy Virgin,[5] who by the bye appeared quite regardless of their supplications, a stiff gale carried us into the harbour to which we were bound; a fact, the knowledge of which was communicated to us by the dropping of the anchor and the furling of the. sails; and these matters having been arranged, we were suffered to emerge from below, twelve at a time, in order to enjoy a little fresh air. It can hardly be imagined of what service this indulgence proved to us, accorded, as it was, for a very brief interval only;—since, that all might in turn be accommodated, each party was obliged to creep back to their den after the lapse of three quarters of an hour. The hatches, however, were thrown open, and other means taken to purify the ships from the putrid effluvia, which night otherwise have occasioned an epidemic; and from this circumstance we derived considerable comfort until, upon evening closing in, we were again pent up and subjected to the same annoyance as before. Two days we continued on board these vessels; at the expiration of which period we were put ashore, and pressed the soil of Majorca, one of the Balearian islands. We entered Palma, its metropolitan town, and here our speculations were excited as to what new adventures should be in store for us. We had done with fear: it was impossible our condition could be rendered worse, and life retained. We were thrown into an old barrack, whose thick and gloomy walls reverberated no

---

5. The uncommon deference and worship paid by Roman Catholics to the Holy Virgin is pretty generally understood; and the instance here mentioned seems principally to prove that Spain has ceased to be a great maritime country; since otherwise the seamen would possess more experience than to put any trust in such dubious mediation. The circumstance is calculated to remind one of the usage of the Turks in this respect,—who, when the wind becomes unfavourable during a voyage or a naval engagement, very rationally proceed to punish the steersman.

sigh; and here, shut out from human observation, our bitter groans were uttered to the ear of Heaven alone. Our garments scarcely sufficed to cover nakedness, hanging about us in rotten shreds, and swarming with vermin, which we ineffectually endeavoured to extirpate, and to the generation of which the air and climate of Spain appear particularly prone.

CHAPTER 4

Cabrera—Prison Island

The endeavours of the Spaniards to induce us to enter their ranks were often repeated; but, notwithstanding the desolate state to which they had reduced us, we were firm in our rejection of their offers, and at length they ceased from troubling us on the subject; but, lest our morsel of food should be eaten for nothing, We were compelled to work for the government: sometimes we laboured in the dock-yards, and sometimes in the construction of new batteries. These modes of employment were not destitute of advantage, since the exercise and the fresh air were calculated to benefit our languid frames, although they, at the same time, most inopportunely sharpened our appetites. We were also thus enabled to make the acquaintance of a great many German soldiers, who belonged to the Swiss regiments which were here in garrison; and amongst these were several who compassionated our forlorn state, and my own in particular. Frequently were they compelled to overlook us while at work; and when the dinner-hour arrived, these humane men gave us a portion of their small allowance; in which act of kindness, also, I was distinguished by them, to the no small jealousy of my companions, whom, in truth, I could not therefore blame. Owing to this good treatment, my health began to be re-established, and the vital energy invigorated. But such a happy state of things did not continue; the Spanish junta having doomed for all French prisoners another place of abode.

In a southern direction from Majorca lies the island of Cabrera,[1] so called because during the season at which it is favourably visited by the rays of the sun, and consequently productive of herbage, flocks of goats and sheep are sent there to feed by the inhabitants of the adjoining Spanish coasts. When, however, either the heat becomes so intense as to dry up the pasture, or inclement winter, with his denizens of frost and snow, reigns over the fields, the desolate little tract is wholly deserted both by man and beast. At the time of which I speak, it happened to be quite destitute of inhabitants, the indolence of the Spaniards inclining them to prefer a more fertile spot.

Such was the place selected as the ultimatum of our destination, in the view that we might there drag out the remainder of our days in destitution and exile. The first division dispatched hither, amongst whom I was myself included, amounted to some few thousands, the miserable remnant of General Dupont's fine army, the remainder of which were either dead, lying in Spanish hospitals, or dispersed in other ways. We were cast upon the shore, in like manner as one of their herds of goats might have been: a guard of Spaniards was set over us; and each man received a supply of bread and vegetables designed to last him several days.

At first, this change of circumstances wore to us an agreeable aspect: we might, at least, wander in the open country wherever we chose; but the cold air soon reminded us, and in no gentle way, of our want of shelter. The ground was bare and desert, a few sprouts of grass only here and there peeping out from the clefts of the rocks which had protected them from the snow-storms. Low shrubs sprung up at distant intervals, from which occasionally a bird was seen to start timidly, as if terror-stricken at the unwonted approach of man. Vaulted by the broad sky alone, and clipped in by the sterile ocean, we seemed to be buried alive. The garrison were lodged in a barrack surrounded by palisades; and as escape appeared to be impossible, they grew quite heedless of our movements: several English vessels were besides cruising near the island, every moment ready to be called in for our destruction in case of the least signs of revolt.

---

1. Cabrera, it is perhaps scarcely necessary to say, is derived from the Latin word *capra*, a goat.

The first night we managed as well as possible, and on the succeeding day assembled in parties, to debate on means for providing lodgement. The first step taken was to break up the underwood and to collect dry leaves. The thick ends of the shrubs were used to stave into the earth in the capacity of rough pillars; but as we were unprovided with tools, our progress was slow and painful and blood perpetually exuded from our fingers and nails. This suffering, however, was held lightly, since it was ourselves, and not our haled task-masters, for whom we laboured. Our intention was, to establish our new colony not far from the sea, near a spring, the only one to be found on the island, but of which the water was brackish in taste: so valuable, nevertheless, was it to us, that we proposed to visit with severe punishment any of our body who should taint it with impurity. To this law the greater portion vociferously consented, while a few heard it in sullen silence. We had no lack of drinking-vessels, and many a one amongst us still retained his military cap, applying it to the purpose of carrying water to the buildings.

In a short time, all was activity. Some of us were incessantly employed upon our structures; others seeking stones upon the seashore which might be converted into rude instruments. Our barracks were erected at proper distances one from another; so that to each household was appropriated a piece of ground, which subsequently, when our arrangements were in a more advanced state, proved of the greatest utility. But there were a few amongst us who took no care for the future, running about wildly, without purpose, like so many savages, and filling their stomachs with any substance, however indigestible, they could procure. These mistaken men were all, within a short period, smitten by the arrow of death.

Summer passed away, and autumn found our works advanced; and we really experienced a sensation of happiness when, on the close of evening, we retired to rest and sleep upon our leafy couches. Suddenly, however, this interval of peace was broken in upon by a new and fearful accident. We had hitherto received our provisions for four days at a time; but it was not uncommon, among thriftless individuals, to see the whole consumed in as many hours, and the remaining period was given over either to the pangs of hunger or to a chance supply. A storm, which lasted an entire week, prevented vessels both from leaving the opposite coast and reaching Cabrera, and consequently there ensued a suspension of our supplies. Daily was the shore thronged with people on the look-out for the arrival of some boat which might rescue us from this dreadful situation; and the weak eyes of the half-starved wretches mistook every giant-wave for the hoped-for treasure. Each little white cloud on the horizon bore the semblance of a sail, until delayed hope made sick the hearts of our unfortunate band. We ran to and fro—to the barracks—to the rocks—to the shore—in search of something wherewith to satisfy our craving hunger, but nothing was to be found. We retorted at length even to the grass and dust of the earth, wherewith to answer the wants of nature; but such things presenting no nutriment, they still pressed upon us. A great many died, and we buried them immediately in the sea, in the horrible dread that, were their bodies to remain before us, the savage longings of the cannibal would arise in our hearts.

A cuirassier was, in fact, killed, for the actual purpose of consuming his carcass, by a Pole, who was in the act of extracting the entrails, when he was discovered by the Spaniards, informed against, and shot. After sentence had been pronounced upon him, he confessed that he had previously done the same by two other of his comrades.

At last, the angry heavens cleared up, and the help which had been so ardently implored came to us. We were all eager to reach the harbour; the provisions were divided without loss of time, and almost as instantly devoured. Our voracity was so keen that the food was swallowed almost without mastication, and hence the indigestible mass produced in several instances immediate mortality: but, so far from feeling any concern hereat, our masters appeared to rejoice at every occurrence of this kind, which left them less to provide for.

A magazine was now constructed for containing a week's

provisions, lest a repetition of the former disaster should embarrass the garrison itself.—Thus the winter went over our heads, and with it much of the gloom and distress which preyed on us, although their remembrance can never be obliterated from our minds. Indeed, if the season had not been mild comparatively with those experienced in other parts of Europe, I think every individual of us must have perished: as it was, the degree of frost which did occur was sufficiently bitter and irritating to poor wretches with scarcely a rag to cover them from its sting.

In the course of the preceding autumn we had gathered together an abundance of dried hay, and had found sometimes, on the shore, a little wood, but not in quantities large enough to keep up comfortable fires. The horse-beans distributed to us were roasted in the glowing ashes, since we possessed no vessels wherein to boil them: in watching this process, our bodies likewise became scorched and smoked, and were hardly distinguishable, in places, from those of black men: but the spring imparted to all new life and activity; and our colony received an accession of strength from the arrival of fresh prisoners, who were brought over in English vessels. Some of these men had not, like us, lost every thing, but still retained supplies both of clothes and money. Many vacancies had been occasioned in our different households by the inroads of death, and these were filled up by the newcomers, each of whom was obliged, on joining us, to contribute, either in garments, cash, or some other thing of value, to the general stock, which articles were appropriated to the poorer members of each party.

When the Spaniards perceived that there was a little money amongst us, many members of the garrison commenced a small trade in bread, cheese, tobacco, and other matters, to us, of luxury. This gave animation to the colony; and several amongst us began to barter for various kinds of seed, saving likewise some of our horse-beans, and proceeding to cultivate our enclosures: hence quarrels arose as to the division and subdivision of this ground, and arbiters were chosen to compose these differences. Thus were the germs laid of future police and courts of justice.

Our endeavours to make the most of our land were happily crowned with success. Our beans came up in the most kindly way; and after this prosperous experiment, we proceeded to plant tobacco, and comforts accumulated around us.

A newly-arrived member of my barrack did a good deal for the enlargement of our convenience: he was a German from Brunswick. H——s had been in the military service of Westphalia; had made a good deal of booty in Spain, and had been fortunate enough to keep a considerable portion of it. He had been stationed near Barcelona, and spoke largely of the bravery of the French troops, and of their success. A gold piece of eight dollars which this man paid us as entrance-money was put to the best purpose, since it not only procured for us several articles of comfort, such as blankets, &c. but likewise fresh supplies of seed; and with the over-plus which remained we bought bread, whereon we banqueted in honour of the founder of the feast.

Since the terrible event of the provision-boat's non-arrival, we had taken care to guard against a recurrence of such danger. We no longer, as formerly, ate our meals in solitude, but clubbed our supplies together, and dined, each household, in concert: hence all waste was prevented, and the common stock held out until the appointed day of replenishment. Subsequently the little enclosure to which my party played husbandmen, furnished us with more produce than we could have possibly anticipated, and enabled us either to afford assistance to our neighbours, or to barter our superabundance in exchange for other commodities.

Each individual applied himself to the manufacture of some necessary article or implement of trade. This attracted the notice of the inhabitants of Palma, who came over, and frequently made little purchases, thereby encouraging our industry, and rendering our prison-colony daily more wealthy and animated.

Everywhere around were spread the seeds of cheerfulness and activity, and it now became possible to distinguish the rich from the poor. Very few suffered privation of any sort; and even in those instances, it arose from their own want of energy and application. The Spaniards themselves took pleasure in the observation of our increasing prosperity.

The temptations formerly held out to us to enlist in foreign service were now renewed both by the Spaniards and English almost every week. They remarked that in no other way were we likely to get free from this irksome captivity, because the war was carried on with the greatest obstinacy on either side. A great many were thus won over, including the larger part of our household: but I and my friend H——s continued inflexible, although his service of Napoleon had been quite compulsory.

Our barrack became by degrees so deserted, that at length we found ourselves alone in it, still pursuing, however, our usual avocations, and feeling tolerably easy. The plan we decided on was to admit no new companions, but to keep ourselves as quiet and undisturbed as possible. Our conversation often turned upon the subject of our respective homes; and particularly when, on a fine evening, we sat upon the turf-seat in front of our barrack, and watched the broad sun decline below the horizon. This is a period especially harmonising with pensive thought; and our minds would at such times wander to far-distant scenes, and commune in imagination with those who, we doubted not, were cherishing for us the same sentiments of affection—the same yearnings of soul.

Two years did we go on thus; during which period we saw a good number both come and go, and many were removed by death. Few lived so regularly, so sociably, and consequently so happily, as ourselves. Some who were too idle to establish and keep up a regular household, were to be seen running about without home or occupation, and almost naked, in different parts of the island—suffering, alternately, the extremes of heat and cold, and becoming finally occupiers of a premature grave.

I have already mentioned that, to ensure the preservation of order, and prevent dishonesty, we had constituted certain umpires over us. These were selected from amongst the oldest and most prudent of our comrades; and subsequently their authority was more firmly established, and recognised by every individual upon the island: it was only the most hardened criminals that we delivered over to the tender mercies of the Spanish garrison. Other arrangements of similar utility were gradually introduced; as, for instance, constables or watchmen, to overlook every thing, and maintain decorum both by day and night. Every owner of property was compelled to take guard in turn, and was held answerable for all the mischief perpetrated during his watch. We also established a regular market for negotiating the sale or exchange of vegetables or other matters: wine-shops were likewise opened.

The Spaniards, seeing us thus caring for the good of our bodies, thought it became them to take heed of our souls; and a priest was deputed to exercise the offices of religion in our colony. This man possessed, however, nothing clerical but his garb: he strove to insult, to disgrace, and to crush us. His opinions were exceedingly liberal, inducing him to confine the favours of Heaven to his own countrymen only, and to denounce us to everlasting perdition because we happened to belong to other nations. In fact, the poor wretch appeared to be so bigoted and ignorant, that he fairly moved our compassion. I will just mention, as an instance of his method of consoling his flock, that upon being once asked when we were likely to be delivered from this captivity, he replied, stamping his stick into the ground, "When this stick shall bring forth leaves, and not before." On another occasion he was more pious, and equally benevolent. We implored his influence to procure us some raiment, of which we were in sad want. His answer was: "Consider the lilies of the field,—they neither sow nor reap, yet our Heavenly Father provideth for them;" and so saying, he turned on his heel, and walked off. Nevertheless, we derived some comfort from his mass-reading on the Sundays which the whole of the prisoners duly attended.

CHAPTER 5

The King's German Legion

Three years had passed, and yet no prospect of the recovery of our liberty. My old comrades, who had originally borne me company to Cabrera, were all dispersed. Many had died broken-hearted: others, tired of this monotonous life, had taken service in the ranks of the Spaniards or English. At length, my friend and I grew weary likewise of our protracted durance, and resolved to take the first opportunity of getting employment: we sickened, however, at the idea of taking part with the Spaniards, and therefore lay out for procuring an engagement in some English regiment, nor was it long before means presented themselves. We received four guineas earnest-money, with the stipulation that we should either serve seven years, or be discharged six months after the conclusion of peace.

We sold our barrack and the adjoining fields to the highest bidder, and spent the piastres which were paid for them in making merry on the occasion of our departure, and drinking farewell to those we left behind. Even this desolate place had spots endeared to us by habit, and which recalled the memory of peaceful, if not happy hours; and we bade adieu to many a little nook wherein we had lain and soothed ourselves with the thoughts of home. Sorrow and suffering had been busy with us during our abode in Cabrera: yet we set about leaving it with heavy hearts and sad faces.

A boat came to conduct us to the English frigate: but before we entered it, a new suit of clothes was given to each of us, consisting of a shirt, a pair of shoes, a woollen jacket, and a military cap. We sprang into the sea, cleaned our persons with sand, bounded lightly out again, and dressed ourselves. Never did I experience sensations so perfectly delightful as those which followed this replenishment of the outer man. A voluptuous irritation, if I may so express myself, spread over my whole frame, and did not subside for several days:—each recruit received, besides, three Spanish piastres in advance of pay.

We leaped into the boat, gave once more to our comrades and to Cabrera an eternal farewell, and glided gently over the tranquil waves towards the frigate, which we reached in a quarter of an hour: directly we were put on board, she got under way.

How different was my situation to that when last I travelled over the briny element! We were now permitted to stay upon deck, and to feel the enjoyment of a sea voyage in favourable weather. The keel of our vessel cut its way swiftly through the waves; and in thirty-six hours, during which we were once or twice in pursuit of other ships, we arrived at Tarragona.

During this short passage, all of us were quite well and comfortable: we had hammocks to sleep in, and our food was wholesome and nourishing, although not exactly plentiful enough to satisfy our voracity, excited by previous privation and the bracing sea air: but it must be remarked, to the honour of the English service, that those engaged in it are very well provided for. The ship was of fifty guns, and had one hundred and fifty hands on board: order and cleanliness reigned in every part: everything was executed with the utmost precision: it was really delightful to behold so much regularity. The sailors appeared to revel in the plenitude of health and strength, and were all neatly dressed and perfectly clean— presenting a striking contrast to the squalid filth of the Spanish sailors, who were ever and anon praying or counting their beads.[1]

---

1. It is remarkable enough that the inhabitants of Roman Catholic countries generally distinguish themselves from those who profess the Protestant faith by an abominable disregard to cleanliness. The immense circle of Germany includes several states of each different persuasion; and any one may observe, upon entering a German village or town, infallible indications of

Having landed at Tarragona, we were conducted to the English depôt, where we became attached to a battalion of the German Legion, then in Sicily. We remained in Tarragona about four weeks, and lived in very pleasant style all the time, our allowance being sixpence a day, with a pound of bread and a pint of wine, the best Alicant being to be purchased for about twopence[2] a bottle.

At the conclusion of the above-mentioned period, arrived a fleet of transport-vessels from Sicily, having on board provisions and other necessaries for the British forces in Spain. The convoy speedily returned with wounded and sick soldiers, and on board one of the vessels we were placed. We did not feel here so much at our ease as in the frigate: in the latter we were considered somewhat as passengers; but now the strictest discipline was observed, and the most trivial fault severely punished. The mariners were, for the greater part, merry and kind-hearted, but rough people, full of frolic whilst the wind was favourable and they had no occasion to work.

As soon as we became a little acquainted with our new service, we were obliged to watch, in company with the sailors, for the preservation of order. The use of water, in so short a voyage, not being restricted, every one was at liberty to drink as much as he chose: but to waste it, by washing therewith, or other wanton expenditure, was decidedly forbidden: it was therefore necessary to guard the casks which contained this precious fluid.

For several days we scudded before a favourable breeze, piercing the brine as an arrow cleaves the air: but subsequently the sky became obscured, thunder-clouds hung overhead, and a storm was evidently approaching: the sea-birds screamed about the masts, and shoals of dolphins floated past our bark, frisking and leaping with unusual glee. We redoubled our caution, binding the sails together, closing the port-holes, arranging the

---

(from previous page) the nature of the prevailing belief. At the same time, as if to counterbalance this disadvantage, it is observable that the Roman Catholic ladies of Germany are, generally speaking, finer and prettier than their Protestant countrywomen.

2. Seven kreuzer, a German coin, thirty-six of which make an English shilling.

pumps, and lowering the topsails. The ocean grew more and more agitated,—the heavens more and more threatening,—the gale tempestuous. Our captain was full of activity. He was here—there—everywhere; and devoted no small attention to the veering of the compass. Our labouring ship was now hurled to the summit of the giant billows, and again sunk into the trough of the sea; now thrown on one of her sides, now on the other:— sometimes a wave broke right over the deck, and drenched all upon it.—I myself was struck down by such a one whilst sitting astern, close by the rudder: it washed me with it to the other side of the vessel, where I lay deprived of all sensation, and half drowned, until another blow brought me again to my senses, thereby enabling me, whilst rolling across the deck, to seize hold of one of the guns.

The bad weather continued to rage, with more or less violence, for some days, and our situation grew extremely critical, because we were not far from shore, and were therefore in great apprehension from the breakers. The mariner, whilst he has plenty of sea-room, feels little anxiety during a storm, presuming his ship to be sea-worthy and his tackle good; and hence it is that few vessels are lost in deep water. Eventually, the atmosphere cleared up, but the swell continued tremendous, which, as is well known, sometimes produces still greater hazard than the preceding storm, the water being left to its own angry mood without counteraction of any other element.

In a short time we came in sight of the steep shores of Corsica. We sailed through the channel Bonifacio, and in a few days afterwards were steering between Sicily and the Italian peninsula. We were enchanted with the view of the Sicilian fields, concerning the beauty of which the sailors, amongst whom were some Germans, discoursed largely, exciting a keen desire in us to witness the country they so highly praised.

CHAPTER 6

Campaigning in Spain

I never, after this period of my life, revisited Spain, and will therefore, ere I quit the subject finally, make the reader acquainted with the peculiarities of those of its towns in which I made some stay.

Madrid and Toledo were the two places which came chiefly under my observation. In the first, my lodging was near the Puerta del Sol,—a spot, the vicinity of which is noted for bringing together persons of the most opposite grades of society: fashionables and plebeians—good and bad—busy and idle—women of virtue and women of pleasure—bigots and bawds—are to be seen parading here at different hours of the day. On one hand you are addressed by a bustling prig of a barber, who offers his services for a few quartos, and while you are undergoing them, proposes to you a fille-de-joie. On the other, you are accosted by a broker, who wishes to know if you will sell your great coat, promising to pay handsomely, and holding the money in his hand. Anon, you become aware of some one dodging your steps; and turning round, perceive an old woman, who, with a look of mystery, whispers to you the virtues of some dozen of her nymphs, declaring them to be fairer and purer than "Our Lady of Atocha." Priests implore alms for the poor in the name of the Deity, casting at the same time lustful glances towards every pretty woman that passes. Honourable ladies make this their place of exhibition, where new dresses are displayed, and every charm of figure studiously set forth; whilst the wretched beggar, who follows them perhaps for a quarter of an hour, departs unrelieved. Every moment offers a change of scene—the objects as various as the presentations of the kaleidoscope.

Our soldiers were, in several cases, great favourites with the fair sex, particularly when their appearance was at all imposing. I have known in some of these bonnes fortunes, instances where even marchionesses and other women of quality have received our heroes in preference to their lawful lords.

Bustle and noise reign triumphant through the whole day in every street. Lemons, oranges, cherries, ham, sausages, meat, bread, wine, brandy, water—in a word, all the necessaries and luxuries of life, are cried about. In every corner chocolate is prepared in the morning, coffee being but little used: the poorer classes are apt to take brandy, of which they can procure the value even of a single quarto. Then come the women with chestnuts,[1] being as black in their persons as so many chimney-sweepers, and annoying every passer-by with the offer of their fruit: I would advise no one, however, to treat these damsels with disdain, because they invariably adopt each other's quarrels, and would fall upon a man in rather a formidable body.

The water-carriers form also a considerable portion of the poorer population, being for the most part foreigners, and gen-

---

1. These ladies appear to have a strong family likeness to the fish-women in Hamburg, who preserve the most intimate alliance with each other, both offensive and defensive: if one is insulted, the whole company conspire together for the purpose of revenging the affront; and the fish-market, on such an occasion, seems overflowing with one universal sound. It is indeed excessively amusing to see and hear the proceedings of these damsels, who spare no violence either of gesture or language towards their supposed enemies—their feelings of honour being particularly acute and sensitive! I myself have frequently, in sportive mood, taken a malicious pleasure in stimulating the angry passions of these heroic ladies, thereby occasioning a good deal of mirth to the standers-by. Shoving their baskets aside, or even casting upon them a look expressive of disdain, is often sufficient to set the whole crew in agitation. In every metropolitan city may be found a class of similar women more or less uncivilized. The *poissardes* of Paris and the Billingsgates of London have precisely the same kind of character; whilst in Copenhagen the fish-women form a body at once barbarous and formidable.

erally robust in person. They are habited in leather, and covered with a large slouched hat: each one of these men has a bucket calculated to hold from forty to fifty quarts, in which they carry water over the town, being paid in proportion to the distance they go and the height to which they bear it in the house. At all the fountains of the town they may be seen assembled in troops, scarce anybody besides resorting thither: hence, we frequently found ourselves implicated in very serious quarrels, when our necessities compelled us to invade what they had acquired the habit of considering as their right. We had plentiful deference paid to us on our arrival, in almost every other respect; but these leathern gentlemen would not budge an inch: they evidently regarded us as so many usurpers; and the office of fetching water, at length, grew dangerous to such a degree, that we felt it advisable to proceed to the fountains in companies, under the escort of an armed patrol.

These water-carriers were extremely active on the revolution of the 2nd of May. They exchanged, on that occasion, the water-pail for the musket; but soon found that the management of the one was by no means so pat to them as that of the other.

Almost the whole day long the bells of the churches are ringing, and processions of every description parading through the city: thus the spectator is constantly reminded of the supremacy of the priesthood and the superstition of the people.[2]

The town of Madrid is pretty well built. There are many fine churches and palaces ornamenting the principal thoroughfares, but the suburbs and smaller streets present few agreeable objects; dirt and dust flying in all directions, and the appearance of the houses being indicative of great want of comfort. The environs

---

2. Processions and ringing of the church-bells are well-known characteristics of every Roman Catholic town, even in the German states, which are certainly far more enlightened than those of Italy or Spain. In England even, a Protestant country, although there are no processions of clergymen and images, the ringing of the bells frequently reminds a foreigner of Catholicism; the only difference being, that the Catholic peals are at any rate harmonious, whilst those of Protestant England, especially in London, are monotonous and discordant to the last degree.

of the city exhibit no pleasant prospects; and if Madrid did not possess the Royal Gardens and the Prado, there would not remain a single place wherein you might find recreation after the heat of the sun.

In a short time after the arrival of our troops, small clusters of booths or stalls were established in front of the several barracks, at which we could purchase dressed or undressed viands of every description, as, for instance, vermicelli, love-apples, rice, tobacco, &c. Every one, in fact, was here able to satisfy his appetite in proportion to his means; the rapacious female trader grasping at the olchavo, in default of obtaining the real; and shouting out, with laudable candour, to attract the customer to her particular standing, "Come here! come here!—Mine is the best! mine is the best!" Many and desperate, indeed, were the squabbles among these amiable ladies, in consequence of their tenacious rivalry.

At Madrid we met with sundry German regiments which were engaged in the Spanish service, and called Switzers. They had been, for the most part, captives taken from the Prussian and Austrian armies, and levied by the Spanish recruiting officers in France at the prisoner-depots. These men were almost wearied to death of their stay here, because they were paid very badly, and treated still worse, and had, besides, no hope of returning to their native country. I met with many brave and worthy men amongst them, who excited my hearty compassion; but my own situation did not admit of my giving assistance to them. We were, however, in the habit of paying reciprocal visits to each other's quarters.

Independently of the inferior payment received by the Spanish soldier, he was dosed with bad bread, and placed in sleeping-rooms filled with vermin. Straw was the material that formed his bed, and the blanket which covered it was of a piece with the other accommodations. Bugs and fleas invaded his rest by regular squadrons, nor was an auxiliary troop of lice by any means unusual. Such was the state of the Spanish royal body-guard—fit preservers of an outworn and loathsome despotism.

It will readily be conceived that these poor fellows, situated thus, would find it necessary to increase their income by every means in their power. Accordingly, they applied their leisure time to various other occupations; some made buttons of bone, some lanterns of paper, others manufactured snuff from ashes and tobacco pounded together in mortars. Again, there were not a few who resorted for the enlargement of their means to tricks more ingenious than respectable; and these, upon being detected, were visited with severe punishment, and exposed to public infamy.

Their dress might have been considered better than their food and treatment—indeed might have been denominated handsome, had they not been obliged to use each suit until it hung about them in tatters, scarcely covering their nakedness. The members of a cavalry regiment which I saw here were habited in long yellow coats, with red facings; huge, uncouth, triangular hats, to which were affixed queues reaching to the saddle; short blue trousers; long white stockings, and shoes with buckles; a very long musket, and still longer sabre at their sides: such were the accoutrements of these chevaliers of the spit, as they were deridingly called by us, in allusion to their clumsy swords. The Spanish troops in Madrid were, indeed, altogether in a most pitiful state; so that when the whole garrison, Spanish and French, were on one occasion reviewed by Murat, he spoke the following words to the general officers around him:—"Here, gentlemen, you may see, at a single glance, the difference between soldiers and no soldiers."

The Spaniards are greatly behind other European nations with respect to the comfort of their inns, and the accommodation of the attendance. The plates and dishes which are placed on the table are generally both dirty and half-broken, and it is not of the least use to remonstrate, since no better are ever to be found. Coachmen and drivers of mules are in the habit of dining on the high road; their fare consisting of cold provisions, which they carry along with them, and which commonly include ham, onions, and garlic; The latter almost always forming an ingredient in a Spanish meal. At the inns on the road they take nothing but wine, and this in moderate quantities and generally diluted. They are by no means nice in respect of lodgings; often sleeping upon the lading of their mules, and crouching down, when the mildness of the season will permit, by the side of the animals themselves, covered by a blanket alone.

Our own situation would have been in no small degree irksome, had we not duly received our payment, and kept each of us a little spare cash. The military post, likewise, frequently brought to different individuals supplies from home; until, among other evils incident to a state of warfare, its operations were suspended. A ration of a pound and a half of bread and half a pound of meat was daily served out to each man; but the former was so mingled with potash that it was scarcely eatable; and as for the latter, it was, in my belief, much oftener the flesh of a jack-ass than of an ox.

It usually happens that the commissariat department of an army is infected with the desire of growing wealthy, and to this the comfort of the unfortunate soldiers is too often sacrificed. Such was the case in the present instance. Our generals and other commissioned officers were treated well enough; but the privates were wholly neglected; nor was it of the least utility to complain, since no notice whatever was taken of any representation of the facts.

The most remarkable building in Madrid is unquestionably the royal palace; but it is situated badly upon an elevation near the walls of the city, no kind of care having been taken to ornament or render agreeable the surrounding ground: on the contrary, its vicinity exhibits almost a perfect desert. The view is, it is true, very fine, towards the park, which is situated about half an hour's walk on the other side of the Manzanares. I believe one of the grandest places of public worship is the church dedicated to our lady of Atocha, in which we assisted at mass every Sunday, fully equipped: this church is not only adorned externally with stonework, but inside are some fine paintings, together with other rarities; besides which, a number of miracles are reported to have been enacted therein. The Royal Hospital, also denominated Hospital for Males, and which was used by the French garrison, is an edifice both extensive and beautiful, and calculated to hold many thousands of patients. I have several times had occasion to look into it, and found it to consist of sundry masses of building very commodiously arranged. It is to be lamented that this noble asylum for disease and suffering should have been so terribly profaned as it was on the second of May: but subsequently, after the French had quitted Madrid for the first time, the Spaniards made even a more melancholy devastation there than our troops had done before: all the French invalids who were necessarily left behind were put to death in the most merciless way, the Spanish military being either too weak or too malicious to interpose for the prevention of such horrors. A person of veracity belonging to our army, who went into the hospital to get cured of his wounds, told me, the fury of the populace was so violent that they actually bored holes through the cheek-bones of these helpless individuals, passed string through the holes, and fastened them thereby to the backs of mules; in this way trailing the wretched sufferers through the town in a sort of triumphal procession, accompanied by shouts and exclamations of savage ferocity from the assembled multitude. It is observable that, in the course of this war, acts of violence were perpetrated of a character to remind the spectator of the scenes said to have occurred at the conquest of South America.

The sanguinary disposition of the Spaniards is indeed sufficiently evidenced in their bullfights, where rich and poor—fashionable and vulgar—sentimental gentlemen and ladies—priests and laymen—all hurry to the arena to behold a spectacle of the most bloody and tyrannous nature. All is, on these occasions, activity and interest, noise and clamour; each man discussing with his neighbour the respective merits of the bull and the matadors, or whatever other designation the human brutes might receive: and the more furious the bull becomes,—the longer the poor animal is subjected to the torture before the finishing blow is given,—the more delighted is the multitude. Ladies and gentlemen nod to the different lighters in token of their approbation, seeming only to fear lest their defined amusement should be at an end too soon. After the scene has come to its close, every one rushes into the arena, eager to gaze upon the convulsed limbs and features of the gallant beast which has been tormented even unto death; but without exhibiting in their own countenances the least spark of feeling. The animal is shortly after removed, and then a fresh fight commences.

During my stay in Madrid, these exhibitions took place usually once a fortnight; and the common talk, during the intervals, was of the last bullfight and the next—of the bravery of the quadrupeds, and the boldness or cowardice of the several matadors.

The Toledo bridge, which I have frequently had occasion to cross over, is another beautiful specimen—indeed quite a chefd'oeuvre, of architecture, and is elevated upon handsome columns; but it cannot fail to strike every one, at a single glance, that this profusion of taste and expense is almost ludicrously misapplied, since the little river over which it is thrown was, during the period of my sojourn, scarcely comparable with a mountain rivulet: in autumn, however, or spring, the Manzanares becomes, by virtue of rain and melting snows, so large, as to bear the appearance of a formidable and unfordable stream. Statues of many of the kings of Spain are introduced by way of embellishment to this structure.

I will conclude the present chapter with a few words touching the city of Toledo. It is at once the most observable and most unfortunate circumstance connected with this place, that it is impossible to procure thereat a good supply of fresh water, which must be brought from a distance of several miles in carts or upon asses, and was very often, in my time there, scarcer and dearer than wine. The town itself is by no means attractive in appearance, looking quite black and sooty, except the cathedral church, which, according to an old tradition, was originally built in honour of a Moorish princess, who had treated with great humanity certain Christian captives;—conduct which, when it came to the ears of her father, procured her a bitter reward for her sweet virtues—reproach and death. Peace to her memory!

Chapter 7

In British Service

I will now take a pleasant spring back again to the Italian sea, and resume the narrative of my adventures. Sicily lay before us; and a favourable wind drove us quickly into the bay of Palermo, our place of destination. The nearer we approached to this town, the steeper became the coast, which at length seemed to rise almost to the clouds, and terminated in the Monte Pellegrino, on which was placed a telegraph, together with a chapel. In this latter edifice was contained the holy picture of some saint, whose name I do not remember, but who was very much given to work miracles by virtue of his canvas representative. In the front of us, as we advanced, was spread the beautiful town above mentioned; to our right, the Monte Pellegrino; to our left, the open coast of the island. It was exceedingly interesting to look towards the port, which was closely strewed with shipping, presenting a regular forest of masts. We continued to glide smoothly over the soft-stirring ocean, and in the course of an hour anchored in the Mola, where the performance of quarantine commences, with which view the constituted officers came immediately to inspect our vessels. Being convinced that the ship's company were all in perfect health, they suffered us the next day to be towed out of quarantine, and we accordingly proceeded as close as possible to the shore. Shortly afterwards came on board the surgeon and officers of our regiment, all of them Germans, who at once treated us with a kindness and courtesy which could not fail to reflect honour upon their native country. Our past sufferings received their hearty commiseration. "Well, my boys," cried the Major, whose name was Soest, "make haste out of the boat; I will soon make proper men of you: if, in four weeks from this, you are not able and ready to spring about like the deer, my name is no longer Soest." We were all enchanted by this good-natured reception, and began to grow quite frolicsome. We came ashore, and now, for the first time after a long and dreary interval, found ourselves once again in military line, performing our various evolutions at the (to us unintelligible) English words of command, which were constantly made use of in the German Legion.

Everybody around us regarded us with astonishment, since in point of complexion, we resembled Africans rather than Frenchmen or Germans; and the question—"What countrymen are they?" was vociferated in every direction. Some took us for Polacks, some for Russians, some for Spaniards, and not a few even did us the honour of believing us to be Turks: thus, accompanied by a large crowd of people, we reached our quarters at San Francisco de Paolo,—a convent, wherein, besides the monks, two battalions of English soldiers were residing, whose devotion was not a jot inferior to that of the holy fathers, which latter indeed was by no means of a formidable character.

Now I was, in truth, an English soldier, receiving both good payment and food; and could perceive, from certain indubitable signs, that I was expanding in proportions every day. To the honour of the English nation, I must say that we were treated in all respects extremely well; and so far from being in want of anything, our comforts were actually superfluous. We were even, for a while after joining our troop, exempted from military exercise, in order to enable us to recover our strength. Several of the new recruits were, in fact, found, on examination, to be in such a state of health as to incapacitate them wholly from service. These poor creatures were in dread lest they should be sent back to their miserable exile; but, on the contrary, they received money enough to carry them, with frugality, to their native homes, together with a necessary supply of raiment, and a regular discharge.

When we were thought to be in sufficiently good trim, our initiation commenced into the preparatory exercises of the English military system. At first, we were drilled an hour, or scarcely so long, each day; so that we grew by degrees accustomed to our new service, and the duty was increased from time to time. This humane treatment recalled to my mind my old original instructors in the art of war, as well as the comforts of my native home, the thoughts of which not unfrequently drew tears into my eyes. The regiment in which I was included, the seventh of the king's German Legion,—consisted chiefly of French prisoners, who were however, generally speaking, Germans by birth: The officers, and the greater part of the Sergeants, formed exceptions to this observation. It had been before Copenhagen; in Portugal, in the battle by Vimiera; and in Spain, in the action of Talavera de la Reina; and in each instance had fully displayed the glory of German valour. By these conflicts, however, its numbers had been dreadfully thinned; and the old remnant was subsequently dispersed amongst other battalions, whilst the staff was sent to England, for the; purpose of forming, out of the recruits levied from amongst the French prisoners, a new battalion. This plan was executed; and after the new regiment had made some stay at Malta, it was ordered to Sicily: the rifle company had been but a little while returned from Spain, where it had been engaged in the War of Liberty, and to this troop I was joined. I received a handsome rifle-gun, and the rest of my equipment was neat and conformable thereto. The whole company, at the head of which was Captain Von S—hardt, with two other excellent officers, was composed of quite young men, the age of no individual amongst us, perhaps, exceeding thirty years. The captain had the privilege of selecting his privates out of the entire battalion, and accordingly made choice only of orderly and courageous men, who were at the same time full of spirit and gaiety, as will appear by the following instance.

A sergeant of the company was condemned to be placed under arrest for four days for an affair of intrigue with the wife of Sergeant F—. The former of these men was very much beloved by our whole troop; and the universal wish was, that he might escape punishment: we, therefore, went in a body to the captain, soliciting a remission of the sentence against H——: but he did not seem at all disposed to concede to our request, particularly as the circumstance had come to the ears of the colonel. We were accordingly obliged to return unsuccessful. H—— went to prison in pursuance of his sentence; but each one of us did every thing which lay in his power to alleviate the inconveniences of his confinement. We likewise designed to give him a joyous welcome immediately on his release, and soon agreed upon the manner of doing so. We decorated the chapel in which he, with eighteen other men, was lodged, with festoons of leaves and flowers: on the table were placed flasks of wine; and when he entered the door, little mortars were fired in honour of his restoration to his comrades. The sergeant was quite overpowered with glad emotion, whilst his rival almost burst with rage, which, however, we did not, trouble our heads about.

After my arrival in Palermo, I became quite an altered man. I had lived four years in the utmost misery and poverty,—I may, indeed, almost say slavery. No other individuals came in my way during this period, if I except my fellow-sufferers, but malevolent Spaniards or formal Englishmen: now, on the other hand, I was the associate of light-hearted Germans, whose gaiety was interrupted, alone, by the duties of their service, and from whom it became, after a short interval, difficult to distinguish the formerly emaciated colonists of Cabrera. Thus much were we changed to our great advantage, reflecting with horror upon the calamities of the last past years, and thanking God for our preservation, and for the happy revolution of our fate.

Sicily, in truth, is one of the few countries which may be called rich, even to superfluity, in the various necessaries and luxuries of human life. Every fruit of the earth is produced in abundance:—oranges, figs, carobs,[1] Indian figs; all sorts of vegetables; wines of the most agreeable strength and flavour: the whole are to be had without requiring the aid of much tillage

---

1. A tree very common in Spain and Sicily.

of the ground, which, if it be but slightly cultivated, returns with tenfold interest the seeds entrusted to its bosom. To counterbalance this prodigality of nature, however, the inhabitants of the country are extremely indolent, using no exertion to make the most of its indigenous advantages. For the last century no improvement whatever has been made in the manners or genius of the natives of Sicily: the same ploughing utensils—the same carts—the same vestments—all continue, and will still continue, at least so long as the government shall remain in its state of reprehensible supineness. I have several times inquired of young, active-looking boys, begging about the streets, for what reason they did not endeavour to get work? to which the universal reply was—"We don't want it: we receive our dinner at the convent of San Dominico, and make provision for other wants as chance directs;" that is to say, they unite the praiseworthy occupations of begging and stealing. The dolce far niente (the sweet trade of doing nothing) is, in fact, highly popular among all classes of the people; and the come sta which salutes your ears at every moment, should be taken literally, as to stand still seems the most delightful enjoyment of a Sicilian's existence. You may constantly see a number of persons sauntering about the live-long day, in order to offer articles for sale which scarcely amount to the value of two or three farthings, their principal object being to overreach you by every means in their power.

For instance, there came one day into our quarters a sans-culotte of this description, who was vending barley-sugar. Jealous of our flesh-pots of Egypt, this pretty fellow was very desirous of helping himself therefrom; but the exercise of all his ingenuity was to no purpose, as there were too many eyes fixed upon his movements. His knavish disposition, however, would not suffer him to depart without doing some mischief; and being foiled in his first attempts, he betook himself to further experiments. He accordingly affected to take leave, but came back almost directly afterwards with a lizard which he had concealed in his bosom; and imagining himself to be unobserved, he threw the noxious animal into one of our kettles. The vengeance of

Nemesis, however, soon made itself apparent in the agency of ten very powerful cooks, one of whom had witnessed the exploit. These formidable personages seized the shuddering miscreant, and holding him tightly, rendered nugatory all efforts to get away: he struggled and kicked furiously; but it was like a small bird in the talons of the eagle, and summary punishment was dealt out in unsparing blows; whilst, in the mean time, one of the cooks had gone to report this occurrence to the adjutant, who came up soon after with two lusty Sergeants, each provided with a suitable cudgel. All supplications for mercy were in vain: they laid the poor devil upon a bench, and inflicted on him twenty-five strokes; by the time he had received ten of which, his small-clothes gave way, and exhibited the seat of honour in its native dignity. Having favoured him with his full amount of lashes, they proceeded to drench their victim with the lizard-soup, which had been meanwhile boiling. The preparation for this excited in his stomach the most furious loathing; in despite of which, however, and of abundant entreaties, wry faces, and deprecations, the obnoxious liquid was forcibly administered. At length he was suffered to hobble away; and never after revisited, to use his own expression, the cursed quarters of the English heretics.

CHAPTER 8

Sicily

During the hot summer days, when it is impossible to get out while the sun is in the heavens, it is customary for the inhabitants of Palermo to recreate themselves by walking in the cool of the evening; and a stranger would be quite astonished to meet a lady or gentleman employed in gnawing a raw cucumber or a head of lettuce, or chewing a bunch of small radishes or a boiled artichoke. These dainties will certainly strike the fair natives of more polished lands as being altogether uneatable: but there, on the contrary, so far from being thought strange, their mastication excites no remark whatever. The southern country people relish these viands extremely; and perhaps there is scarcely an individual in the whole kingdom of Sicily who understands the method of, dressing a German cucumber-salad.[1] When we once ordered such a thing in a certain wine-shop, the landlord brought us unpeeled cucumbers, each cut into four pieces, over which were sprinkled oil and vinegar: angry at this blunder, we instructed the man how to rectify it; but he frankly answered, that he never in his whole life had made, nor would he now begin to make, such a hog's mess.

When the simple green lettuce is used by them as a salad, the common people may frequently be seen plucking off one leaf after another, and dipping it in vinegar and oil by way of dressing; whilst to the higher classes, it is served on a plate at table, each individual being left to qualify it with the accompanying condiments of vinegar, oil, and pepper, according to his own peculiar taste.

---

1. Cutting it into slices, in the usual English way.

The most favourite dish of all is macaroni, which are preferred to any thing else by the Italians, whether fashionables, working people, lazzaroni, or, in short, to whatever grade of society they may happen to belong. They are made in a variety of different shapes; either resembling great or little stars, or snails, or minute threads, even as thin as a hair, in which latter form they are generally most admired; and in every public-house, the saucepan is in readiness to receive them until a late hour at night.

Macaroni are to be had in greater or less quantities, at the option of the purchaser, who takes them into the first public-house he comes to, and claps them into any disengaged saucepan or kettle in his way, without questions asked on either side. While his macaroni boil, he goes to fetch his Parmesan; and when they are ready, he lays one stratum on a plate, scraping the cheese over it, then again macaroni, then again cheese, in alternate layers, until the whole is amalgamated. This being accomplished, he takes a piece up in his fingers,—the macaroni, which are very long, reaching from the plate to his mouth; and whilst his meal is in progress, the smacking of the tongue and sparkling of the eye indicate the gusto with which it is devoured. A glass of wine still further improves its relish; and the game of la more [2] is often played by a party of boon companions over their macaroni, the loser being paymaster of the whole entertainment. This

2. La More is a game played with great earnestness and frequency in almost all the southern countries of Europe except Greece, where I never saw it practised: it is played chiefly in the public houses and open streets; and generally, though not always, for some trifling wager. Two persons are commonly the number engaged; and both of these raise and bend back the right arm, immediately stretching it out again, and loudly crying any given number,—at the same instant extending one finger, or more, or none. These out-stretched fingers of each antagonist's hand are then reckoned together; and if their number agrees with that called out by either party, (provided both have not fixed upon the same, in which case it is a drawn game,) a point is counted, and marked by the extension of one finger of the left hand; and he who first, in this way, has all the left-hand fingers held up, wins the stake, whatever it may be, for which they are gambling. This simple game is generally practised with infinite spirit and interest, and attended with violent gesticulation; the gist of the diversion depending upon the celerity and simultaneousness of the movements of both parties.

kind of gambling is very frequently productive of quarrels, not seldom ending; in bloody arbitrament, and even in murder; and although the police is on the alert in all directions, it is too weak to prevent a recurrence of such scenes.

Another favourite dish of the Sicilian people is the Indian fig,[3] which grows here, as I have already observed, in great abundance. This plant is used as a sort of enclosure for gardens and meadows, and some of its leaves extend from three to four feet in diameter, bearing each an innumerable quantity of rough-looking fruit, which is large and coloured like the castanos, being spread with similar spots, upon which are prickles sufficiently sharp to penetrate the surface of the skin, and subtle to lodge under it. I was once smartly punished for my ignorance of this. Some of my comrades were with me in a garden wherein a great many of these figs were growing: one of the party, a facetious sort of fellow, seized quickly hold of a fig, and put it into his mouth with the action of biting it, proposing to me to do the same. He praised the agreeableness of its taste and flavour; and I was at length persuaded: but scarcely had I touched the fruit with my tongue, before I cast it from me with a sharp cry; yet even in that short interval, it left behind it a host of stinging prickles, which incapacitated me from eating with any comfort for the space of seven or eight days. If, however, you begin by cautiously opening the peel, you will find within a yellow mass, containing many hard kernels, and this part of the fruit is so delicious as to incite you to eat even thirty or forty. It is not every one, however, who can open the shell or rind dexterously; and an awkward hand will inevitably suffer more or less inconvenience from the host of prickles which seem purposed to defend the fruit. The traders in this article, therefore, open it themselves for the purchaser, before whom it is exhibited on plates, four or six of the figs making a lot, for each of which they charge a bajocco.[4] The method of opening them is with a sharp knife, the fingers being protected by three thimbles made of reed—one on

---

3. Called by the botanists cactus.
4. A coin about the value of a halfpenny.

the thumb, one on the fore-finger, and one on the middle finger. The fig is unclosed by one cross-cut, and two more at each end of it, and thus its inside is extracted without having been at all touched by the operator's hand. Scarcely do I recollect any other eatable which can be taken with so great zest; and as cleanliness is, in this country, a pearl of great price, the very circumstance of the knife being steeped in water between the un-closing of each fig, actually gives an additional stimulus to the appetite. Even wealthy and fashionable persons will not object to enter the little booths of the fig-sellers, and regale themselves to the value of two or three grani.[5]

In every principal thoroughfare of the town, there are likewise standings for people who vend lemons and oranges, which fruits are seen piled thereat in the most luxurious profusion, and swelling with juice, presenting a delightful object to the passer-by. Gold and silver fish gambol in handsomely-shaped glass reservoirs, to increase the temptations of each booth, and in the evening the whole are brilliantly illuminated. Hence, a walk through the streets of Palermo towards night is exceedingly amusing, and into whichever of these booths you chance to stroll, a pretty-looking girl salutes you by her offers of attendance.

The streets themselves are handsome, and the buildings tasteful; but little, if any care is taken to keep either neat and clean. In summer, and in dry weather, the gardeners cross the streets with asses, and gather up the dust in baskets; but in the winter-time, the inhabitants are in no small danger of being suffocated by this article, in spite of the paved cart-road. The flag-stones on either side are irregular in breadth, and in some streets altogether wanting. Tradesmen, alone, inhabit the ground-floor, where their shops are situated, but the superior classes would deem it discreditable to reside so low. The ground-floors even of the houses of the nobility are commonly let to working-people and others of the very poorest description, and the entrances of these rooms have no connexion whatever with the apartments above. Thus, under one and

---

5. A grane is about the value of a halfpenny.

the same roof, you may often find the excess both of luxury and destitution:—half-naked children may be seen crawling round the princely equipage of the nobleman who inhabits, in common with them, the same dwelling, and who is just about (hemmed in by his richly-liveried domestics,) to enter his carriage, not deigning to notice in the least his forlorn fellow-lodgers. Upon the exclamation guarda! the coachman lashes forward his horses, quite regardless of any poor devil whom he might possibly trample into the dust.

Convents literally swarm both within and without the town. The upper floors of the street called Toledo are provided with trellised windows, behind which are immured the victims of parental fanaticism; new-born children even being frequently devoted to the cloister by their misguided mothers. Boys of six years and under are to be met walking, dressed in the habit of the convent to which they are destined, and led by the holy fathers; and girls of a similar age, and attired with vestments of a similar nature, parade about under the chaperonage of the abbess or elder nuns. Mendicants of the Franciscan or Capuchin fraternities are crossing the streets every here and there, bearing in their hands reliquaries or figures of saints, which they submit to the salutations of the faithful; and after a while these articles wear so be-slobbered an appearance, that a tolerably strong stomach is requisite in the devotee to enable him to add his quota of kisses: the trade is a thriving one, however, on the part of the priests; and it is but seldom that a true-born Sicilian declines to add his homage to that of his predecessors; all which turns in remarkably well to the purpose of the image-bearer, since the act of worship is uniformly accompanied by the dropping a few bajocci into the box attached to the reliquary.

These mendicants also not only exhibit but sell their statuary and relics. One presents you with remnants of the garment of a male or female martyr, which he declares to be a specific against toothache, headache, and in short, all other diseases incident to the human frame, So many clothes, indeed, are hawked about, professing to have originally belonged to the same individual saint, that it would seem they were each in the habit of keeping a prodigiously large wardrobe.

In most of the chambers of the monks, great disorder and want of cleanliness are apparent: and many of the priests present figures disgustingly filthy. In our quarter, namely the cloister or convent of San Francisco de Paolo, we lived in very familiar intercourse with the fathers; one of whom was extremely desirous to extend the sphere of his benevolent intimacy so as to include our wives, endeavouring to establish an intrigue with the spouse of one of our grenadiers. He flattered himself on being in the way to attain the full accomplishment of his wishes: but, whether through fear of discovery, or real virtuous constancy to her husband, (which latter sentiment by the bye is not very common amongst the wives of soldiers,) the lady unfolded to her legal possessor the whole affair; and he being a cunning fellow, concerted with his wife that she should continue to hold out hopes to the lustful priest of his being made perfectly happy at a certain understood hour—warning him, at the same time, to beware of her jealous and watchful husband. The monk, in the fullness of his exultation, promised every thing; and appointed a rendezvous in an old ruinous chapel at some distance from the convent; in the middle of which chapel was an aperture through which might be perceived the coffins underneath. According to this appointment, the parties met; but had hardly arrived at the place, when the husband darted forth from his ambush. He seized hold of the interloper by the throat, and demanded in rough terms of the trembling culprit, what he was about to do with his wife? To this interrogatory, no answer was returned; upon which, the soldier professed himself resolved to expose to the eyes of the public at large this sanctified libertine. Our holy father was now touched: he began to implore pity in the most abject terms; offering his purse and his watch if the other would suffer him to depart. My comrade made as if he was altogether deaf to these entreaties, and affected to grow more and more furious: after awhile, however, he appeared to relent; pocketed the proffered valuables; and returned home with his cara sposa, to enjoy a hearty laugh at the expense of the disappointed gallant.

In the autumn, I witnessed a spectacle to me perfectly novel, consisting of a public festivity of the natives. Walking one day upon the shore, near to the Garden of Flora, I saw innumerable crowds of people assembled, not only parading on the shore itself, but filling a quantity of boats which ran immediately along the coast, and which were provided with guns, discharged every moment into the air. On arriving nearer, I perceived that these shots were aimed at huge flights of birds, which were just migrating to this island from the continent of Europe—swallows, starlings, and other birds of passage. I cannot describe the delight which was manifested by the multitude at the destruction of these poor animals; the atmosphere resounding with their triumphant acclamations. "Ah! poor little creatures!" thought I to myself, "in my country you may have escaped many a hazard; and here, after a perilous travel, when approaching near your journey's end, you are slaughtered in the mere spirit of idleness:" for I observed that they were none of them picked up, except indeed by the ducks, who seemed to gobble them in with prodigious avidity.

The Lent dishes of the Sicilians are not found here in such great profusion as might be expected; the people giving as a reason the existence of so many convents, in every one of which a good deal of fish is daily consumed. Shellfish, however, is more plentiful, consisting of lobsters, shrimps, and polypi; and it is amusing to see two or three hundred fishing-smacks, both within and without the bay, plying their trade in the middle of the night. On each boat are several candles, or torches, by which the harbour is perfectly illuminated: and by this light the finny tribes are attracted, thus falling a readier prey to their merciless captors.

The environs of the Sicilian metropolis present many beautiful views, particularly in the direction of the Monte Pellegrino, where a good many elegant villas and gardens are to be found. Here are situated the summer-houses of most of the patricians; and the king, during his residence on the island, also preferred this neighbourhood to any other whatever. I often met his majesty riding hither on horseback, attended by a single servant only. Although very little liked by his subjects, this monarch was in the habit of traversing unguarded the streets of Palermo, being scarcely noticed by any one, and those whom he did encounter merely saying, as he passed,— *"Il Re!"* and hardly touching their hats. Quite different, however, was the scene when a procession appeared: every one fell immediately upon his knees, how dirty soever it might happen to be; and I really think, had any individual declined to pay this homage, he would have incurred the hazard of compulsion, and that in no gentle way.

The stranger, in common with the native, is annoyed, in this beautiful country, by many species of inconvenience. The former, in particular, should be strictly upon his guard; because, however brave a Sicilian may possibly be, he is seldom untainted with the spirit of treachery,—which disposition, in fact, he does not appear anxious to conceal. At several times, our muskets were stolen even from the sentry-posts; and in truth, no foreigner should place in them any degree of confidence, since they cannot be faithful one to another, and much less are to be considered trustworthy by such as differ from them in language or belief. The least affront causes them to clutch their poniard; and if prevented from gratifying revenge on the spot, they follow up their victim with unrelenting ferocity.

One day, a soldier named Haupt was promenading on the shore; and having washed his small-clothes, was drying them upon his shoulders, when a Sicilian, who was passing, came on him before he was aware, seized the garment, and ran off. Haupt pursued him, and, crying out for assistance, was joined by some of his comrades who were near the spot: they overtook the thief, rescued the stolen trousers, and punished him as he deserved. The Sicilian became possessed by the demon of revenge; and sought, without ceasing, for an opportunity to gratify it against his original antagonist, whom he at last found in a lonely spot doing duty as sentinel. Rushing treacherously upon the unsuspecting soldier, he struck him repeatedly with his accursed knife, and the poor fellow was thus precipitated into another state of existence by the cowardly act of a ruffian who was his original aggressor. Upon the arrival of the party who came to relieve guard, they found their unfortunate messmate robbed and murdered, and a scrap of paper lying by him, on which was written *Questo e por gli pantaloni.*[6] In this manner is the vindictive temper of these islanders displayed, not alone to foreigners, but to others, of their own country. The most atrocious excesses, including assassination, may often be traced to the most trivial causes: indeed, the Sicilian blood boils a hundred times quicker than that even of the neighbouring Italians—resentment of supposed insult raging more powerfully than amongst any other European people; and even should the arm of public justice be called in to avenge them upon their enemy, the expiation is frequently deemed insufficient.

---

6. So much for your trousers!

CHAPTER 9

Serpents in Paradise

This very beautiful country is also subject to other annoyances. Poisonous reptiles abound therein, against which every body should be placed upon their guard. Serpents from six to eight feet in length, scorpions, tarantulæ, and other reptiles, are found in large numbers. Thus, one fine morning, while I was in my little room at the hospital, where, besides myself, three other sick persons were accommodated, we were all of us enjoying the fresh breeze introduced through the open window, which commanded both a fruit and a kitchen-garden. Happy in the sensation of returning health, and regaling ourselves each with a pipe of tobacco, we contemplated with delight the trees burthened with lovely blossoms and delicious fruit, and which exhaled the most aromatic odours: a desire seized us to taste some of these luxuries; and we comforted ourselves by the reflection, that our approaching discharge from the hospital would enable us to gratify this appetite. Suddenly a loud hissing at the window excited the attention of the whole party; and a large black viper, followed closely by another, glided swiftly along the opposite wall. The two almost immediately commenced a furious battle; both animals twisting their folds round each other with such violence, that we could almost distinguish the crackling of the joints, although the smoothness of their long bodies soon enabled them to disengage themselves. They reared themselves aloft; renewed their convolutions; fell back again upon the earth; commenced and recommenced their conflict; and thus the light continued several minutes. One was evidently weaker than the other, and made perpetual efforts to escape; but could not. for awhile accomplish her desire, being always stopped by the enemy. At length, however, she got away, and precipitated herself into a pond or basin of water which lay in the garden underneath, and was used to water the plants. The other lost no time in following, and had overtaken her antagonist, when both were suddenly lost to our view. After some moments, the stronger one re-appeared, trying, with all her might, to spring over the edge of the basin, which was finally accomplished: she crept back slowly to the scene of the contest, and lay basking in the sun. The battle had manifestly fatigued her much, as was palpable from her forked tongue hanging out of her mouth, whilst in several parts of her body wounds were visible. Until now, we had observed the action and its result in silence: and having suffered her to rest awhile, we sought about for large stones, and threw them forcibly upon the reptile. Some of these hit the mark, but not sufficiently hard to do her any considerable injury. She now retreated with all dispatch into her lurking-place; and after a few minutes came up the owner of the garden, to whom we related what had passed. "O!" said he, "I know these gentlemen: they are great enemies to my vegetables." He took his stick, and pulled with it the viper which had been suffocated by the water, from out the pond: she exhibited still a few signs of animation, but was quickly destroyed by blows.

A few days afterwards I quitted the hospital, during my stay in which, I was given to understand that invalids were often annoyed by serpents, even in their own rooms. I myself frequently encountered them in my walks, as they lay by dozens in bushes and in hedges, on the look-out for prey. Their skins were beautiful in the extreme, often resembling ribands of the most glowing hues. A comrade of mine was once in the act of grasping one of these supposed ribands, and would have smarted sadly for his blunder, had it not been for my timely intervention.

Scorpions, likewise, abounded in such large numbers, that the soldiers frequently discovered them both in their knapsacks and bread-baskets: we were therefore obliged to prepare scorpion-oils, which alleviated the pain of their sting. These are composed of scorpions themselves, which are put into a little bottle full of olive oil; the heat of the sun decomposes the scorpions, and hence they become thoroughly amalgamated with the other essence. By one of these loathsome and even terrible reptiles I was once exceedingly frightened. We were fetching bullets from Castelamar, and amongst them was a scorpion which was in the act of darting at my breast: I stepped back, however, in time to prevent the favour designed for me.

The Sicilians were in the habit of making a circle of powder, within which they placed the scorpion, taking it up with the tongs, and afterwards setting it on fire; by which means the insect was of course destroyed. They likewise make circles of glowing coals, in the middle of which the scorpion is put, its terrors and sufferings occasioning inconceivable pleasure to the lookers-on: the poor devil, first with quick action, which pain soon renders slower, runs round the ring, retreating by degrees to the centre, till it is ultimately killed by the fierce heat. In no instance, however, had I opportunity to authenticate what has been frequently stated as a fact by others, namely, that the scorpion is accustomed to terminate its existence by its own sting. During my stay in Sicily, a single instance only came within my knowledge of any man having been killed by a scorpion—and this was a member of our artillery corps, The reptile had concealed itself in one of his shoes; and when, on rising in the morning, he put his naked foot therein, the sharp pain of the sting induced him to withdraw it hastily, and on searching, the cause of the evil soon became apparent. Not, as it unfortunately happened, being aware of the danger of such an occurrence, it was disregarded by him, and he went about his business. After a while, however, finding the pain grow more and more acute, and the foot rapidly swell, he began to think seriously of the matter, and was advised to consult a medical man. The surgeon examined and probed the wound; but the poison having by this time been taken up by the absorbents, the whole economy of the system was vitiated, and no effectual aid could be administered. Thus the poor fellow lost his life, and the service a brave and worthy soldier.[1]

Besides vipers and scorpions, quantities of tarantulæ were occasionally beheld by us: but I was equally unfortunate here as in the case of the scorpions, since the Tarantular Dance was never exhibited in my presence.[2] To look upon these creatures, however, was quite enough to produce terror and shuddering.

Thus rolled on the days in sadness or in mirth; and many of them were well-nigh consumed in ardent aspirations after our native land. Neither the esteem of my officers, nor the friendship of my comrades, both of which, I rejoice to say, I enjoyed, could repress my longing to change the military for the domestic life; but it was necessary to exercise the quality of patience, as was confessed, in their despondence, by a number of other anxious hearts, who, like me, languished for home, and who cursed the day on which they left it to follow a life of toil and bloodshed. So powerful was this sentiment, that some amongst us sought to gratify it by desertion; others by mutilating themselves; but not one of these succeeded in accomplishing his object. One day I was in the barrack-court, wherein were placed three companies of our battalion, when I heard a shot fired near me, which was followed the next minute by a terrible cry, and "O, my God!" was

---

1. Scorpions are certainly found in great quantities in Sicily and the southern parts of Italy, but very seldom in the northern districts of the latter country. Their abiding-places are principally fixed in lumber-closets, behind loose pieces of wainscoting, and in cloacœ. I have some reason, however, to think that they are neither so numerous nor so dangerous as the accounts of certain travellers would lead us to imagine. 2. Tarantulæ are not so commonly to be met with, but they are by far more noxious reptiles than scorpions. The author, it seems, never witnessed an example of the maddening effects of their sting; but I can myself bear testimony (though not, I am thankful to say, in my own person) to the veracity of such results. The individual whom I saw thus wounded, began soon after the accident to caper about in the most furious manner, until, quite exhausted by the violent exercise to which he had unwillingly been subjected, he sank down in complete stupefaction.

vociferated by a number of voices. A soldier of the barrack-guard had shot himself through the hand, for the purpose of disabling himself; but he repented of his act when too late: the hand was quite dashed to pieces, and it became necessary to amputate it, together with the fore-arm. The circumstances of this man were, in every respect, peculiar. He possessed a settled notion that he was a natural son of the Duke of Gotha, in which idea he strengthened his belief from day today. Hence arose a great feeling of pride, by which he was induced often to address his officers with a good deal of arrogance, and which eventually tempted him to endeavour by mutilation to get free from his humble situation. As I have already stated, this kind of conduct was altogether ineffectual, although practised every succeeding week.

In order to employ the time, which was by no means fully occupied, our men resorted to a great many different artifices.—In the court of the barrack was a bakehouse, which however was not used as such, but as a stable. One of the cloister cats, a very large fat animal, having lost her way, came across the court. Myself and some others, who had witnessed puss's entrance, immediately commenced a pursuit, in order that we might catch and dress her. We pressed her pretty closely, but she somehow or other eluded us, and took refuge in the bakehouse, which was instantly placed in a state of blockade. On the one side we pushed in a long stake, and at the other a large sack was held open before a hole, for the purpose of receiving our victim, should she run that way. We reckoned, however, without our host: Grimalkin, far too prudent to commit herself thus, lying by snugly at the back of the building. Our deliberation as to further measures was not protracted. A wisp of burning straw was thrown in, and the cat, terrified at the idea of conflagration, made a bolt at the hole, and, as luck would have it, sprang right into the middle of the sack, where she met with instant death. The skin having been removed, her carcass was cut into pieces, was soaked twenty-four hours in vinegar, and anointed with garlic and honey until all the disagreeable strong flavour was subdued, after which it formed a capital fricassee. We were all of us sufficiently accustomed to this sort of cookery, having had a good deal of experience thereof in Spain, where many a pretty little kitten suffered the same fate. We spared nothing calculated to give relish to our dish;—neither pepper, black or cayenne, black bread, &c. When it was all ready, we drew round the table, in great good-humour, and began our meal, not forgetting the accompaniment of a few bottles of wine. It so chanced that the wife of our Sergeant entered: for this woman we entertained a very high respect, several of us having been redeemed by her mediation from the malevolent complaints of her husband. To a question from her as to the particular nature of our viand, we replied that it was a cony; and accordingly she seated herself with the intention of picking a bit: in fact, she ate with great heartiness, and did not decline to lubricate her mouthfuls with a glass or two of wine, which had rendered us all, especially the trumpeter, unusually gay. Dinner being finished, the latter left the room, and returned to it bringing the skin of the cat, which had in the mean time been stuffed with straw, and which he threw upon the table, shouting these words, "Look, Mrs. Sergeant: here is the hide of our Sicilian cony." The good lady became so horrified hereat, that we grew afraid lest she should be ill; and from that time forward, the poor trumpeter was no longer one of her favourites. To be serious;—I can assure my readers, that the flesh of a well-fed cat is extremely good: it is indeed (presuming her to be properly dressed,) not only agreeable in taste, but actually dainty; and it is imagination and prejudice alone which protect the feline race amongst us from the uses of the gastronomic art. The same prejudice obtains in Germany with respect to the raven, which is scarcely eaten by any one there without a feeling of disgust, whilst in France they can be purchased in every market. Thus, also, in the ship wherein I voyaged from Spain to Sicily, the cook was in the practice of eating, almost every day, roasted mice, certainly not from scarcity of other meat, but as a matter of preference.

The lower classes of Sicily are likewise very fond of dried beans, and pease roasted upon the coals; either of which may be obtained at any wine-house. Plates-full of beans, boiled in salt water, may be purchased at the corner of every street. All sorts of entrails, hardly submitted to purification by water, are roasted upon the coals, and eaten by the common people without the slightest disgust. They even collect from the streets old bones of meat, which they boil, using the fat to qualify cakes made from the flour of Turkish wheat: and every where around you hear the cry of "hot, hot, quite hot!" and a great many hungry mortals are to be seen in crowds enclosing these public frying-pans from morning to night. Snails, both in the shell and out, and polypi, are swallowed with infinite gusto; in short, I never in my life saw such an odd assemblage of eatables as is patronised by the good citizens of Palermo.

Innumerable goats are driven in herds each morning into the town; and these animals know perfectly well at what houses they are accustomed to be milked; so that they halt, of their own accord, at the proper spots. During the operation, the goat-herd cries, with a hoarse voice, in order to attract the attention of purchasers, "Milk, milk! fresh, warm, fat milk! milk from the mountains—buy! buy!"—Each animal has, depending from his neck, a small bell, the music of which is, when they tinkle in concert, not inharmonious. As soon as the goat-herd has satisfied his customers, he takes the bagpipe, which hangs at his neck, and plays a little tune with it, not very delightful to German ears.

With respect to the female sex, I must observe, that we Germans were very much favoured by its fair members. A good many of us reaped abundant laurels in the sports of Cupid. But we were obliged, at the same time, to exercise great caution; because, if the husband by any chance discovered the intrigues of his wife, the cicisbeo would run the hazard, if not on his guard, of getting an unlucky thrust with the poniard. A sergeant of our regiment, a remarkably fine young man, had been implicated, for a considerable time, in an intrigue with a lady of rank, from whom he received a number of presents; and every one expressed surprise at the luxurious way of his living, as it was evident that his pay bore but a very small proportion to his expenditure. One day when he had crooked his elbow a little too much, the secret was let out; and one of his comrades, who possessed some knowledge of the lady's spouse, hastened to his palace and discovered the whole transaction, in hope of obtaining a reward. A little while after, the unfortunate sergeant was found murdered in an obscure alley.

Women of pleasure haunt the streets of Palermo in inconceivable numbers; and several amongst our troops carried back to their native country souvenirs more enduring than agreeable of their fascinating society. Communication with these ladies is rendered additionally facile by the intervention of numerous procurers, both male and female, who offer their living wares in a manner completely destitute of coyness; by which description of traffic, however generally the pleasure may be distributed, the profit is almost wholly shared between these respectable persons and the surgical practitioners, who are many of them in the habit of inscribing over their doors, *aqui il cura il mal venereo.* In fact, this proclamation is hoisted, in one or more instances, in every street.

Several members of our regiment married Sicilian women; commonly, however, from the very dregs of the people, who, devoted to every imaginable and unimaginable vice, appeared to be quite unsusceptible of the least good. They were, in short, so many disgraces to their sex; not capable of preserving fidelity to their husbands even for a single week; on the contrary, ready to barter their favours for a trifle with any who were fools enough to purchase them.

Thus, for instance, a very brave and well-behaved soldier, by name Linden, unhappily contracted marriage with a wench of this character. She had contrived to inveigle him to such a degree, that he at first put faith in all her expressions: but subsequently he learnt that he possessed merely the name of husband, whilst the virtual honours of that title were awarded to a certain sergeant. For some time the poor deceived man felt a good deal of uneasiness, particularly as he was unable to obtain any positive proof. One night, however, that he was upon guard, a furious attack of jealousy drove him home, where he discovered his rival cradled in the arms of his abandoned wife. Drawing his sword, he sprang upon the de-spoiler of his honour: but the weapon glanced aside upon the rib of the miscreant, who as quick as lightning darted from the bed, and succeeded in escaping out of the house. The circumstances of the case were suppressed; and the interloping sergeant professed to have received his hurt by a murderous attack of the inhabitants.

CHAPTER 10

Napoleon Falls

I cannot as yet bid *adieu* to the remembrance of our various amusements in Palermo. We had taken an apartment near our quarters, where we spent almost every evening in company, at least when not prevented by military occupations. Here we danced, and sang, and drank, and, in short, perpetrated all kinds of festivity. German and Sicilian dances were alternately practised—the latter being taught us by native ladies, who were anxious to take part in our merriment. With this exception, no one was permitted to come amongst us, unless introduced by a member of our own corps; which regulation was indeed frequently opposed by soldiers belonging to the other battalions, who several times attempted to gain entrance by force, but always in vain. At no time were we on a kindly footing with the third and sixth regiments of the German Legion; and therefore individuals attached to these corps were exempted from the privilege of being brought in by a friend. This exclusion was never forgiven; and the parties against whom it was levelled were perpetually seeking opportunities of revenge. The senior of our company, a good-natured fellow of thirty-six, who was a general favourite with both officers and privates, was one evening, whilst we were indulging ourselves with mirth and wine, in a neighbouring public-house close to our apartment, enjoying the lively conversation of his sweetheart. Suddenly twelve men, belonging to the rifle company of the third battalion, entered the place; and falling upon him, although he had not given the slightest provocation, proceeded to treat him exceedingly ill. In self-defence, he snatched up a sword, and vowed he would kill the next man who should touch him,—a threat which he would undoubtedly have put in practice, not in any degree wanting courage: his determined look and gesture made his cowardly assailants pause, and they debated between themselves in what manner they should endeavour to secure him. Accidentally one of our men passed the house; and the terrified girl, her eyes full of tears, reports to this man that a soldier of the seventh regiment is on the point of being slain. Immediately on receiving this intelligence, he hastens to give us the alarm; and each individual, starting to his sword and cap, rushes impetuously to the opposite wine-shop, which is soon abandoned by the enemy. In the commencement, fists alone were the weapons made use of; but shortly swords were plucked from their scabbards, and a regular battle ensued, in which many wounds were inflicted on either side. Fresh members of both battalions now came up half-naked from the barracks, with fixed bayonets: and in the dark night it was scarcely possible to distinguish friend from foe. Confusion indeed reigned triumphant. The third battalion had a good many men wounded; we, on the other hand, only a few.

Patrols were at length dispatched in every direction throughout the town; and numbers were conveyed to the guard-house, which was soon quite filled; the conflict being ultimately terminated by the dispersion of all the combatants.

On the next morning, an order of the day was put forth by our brigadier, in which we were reproached for want of harmony; and it was strictly forbidden for the soldiers of the two obnoxious battalions to enter at one time the same wine-house. On the side of the enemy several swords were missing,—the worthy owners thereof having preferred throwing them away to using them courageously: however, be it remembered, these fellows were amongst the twelve who had originally occasioned the dispute.

A report reached us that the army of Napoleon had been beaten in all directions. Shortly after, we received the news of his abdication and exile to Elba; as also the intelligence of peace having been concluded with France. The exultation hereupon was universal, since it now appeared quite certain that we should speedily be discharged, according to the terms of our capitulation. But we were again disappointed; as the English government, in spite of the restoration of peace and downfall of Buonaparte, seemed incredulous of the stability of the present state of things; and in the exercise of this incredulity, subsequent events proved them to have been wise. After some interval, appeared a few French vessels bearing the white flag; and shortly after, a naval detachment, consisting of a frigate and several brigs, which arrived from Elba, landed their seamen, who seduced many of our soldiers to go with them on board, and these, of course, never returned. It was easy to observe, that the commanders of these ships were more the agents of Napoleon than of the king.

Not long after the departure of the frigate and her companions, we received news of the flight of the Emperor from Elba, and that Murat, then king of Naples, had acknowledged him; which occasioned orders for us to proceed to Milazzo, a town appointed as the rendezvous for those troops which were destined to assist the restoration of Ferdinand IV. to his peninsular monarchy. With infinite satisfaction did we take leave of Palermo, of which place we were heartily tired; and bade adieu, with well-feigned emotion, to our various sweethearts, whom we buoyed up with expectation of our speedy return—a catastrophe which we were particularly desirous to avoid. The boats came up: we sprang with renewed vigour into them, and speedily reached the ship, which instantly put off to sea. Our passage occupied but a few hours; and under a favourable wind, we shot into the bay and harbour of Milazzo.

Here were already assembled a considerable quantity of troops, English as well as Sicilian; and every day brought fresh reinforcements. The Sicilian forces were burning with desire to measure arms with the Neapolitan macaroni, and longing for the period of embarkation.

Milazzo has an old castle, reduced to a perfect ruin; and it was garrisoned by a single regiment. It is defended by walls, but cannot be considered a strong fortress, as is represented by M. Blaquiere. On one side it is washed by the sea, on the other it is bounded by an un-fertile and sand-covered plain.

We found here extremely good and cheap wine, but nothing else in the least degree remarkable.

At length, the wishes of the Sicilians were accomplished. Six thousand men, partly of that country and partly British, were embarked to accompany the king, who came to us on board an English vessel: he was saluted by the whole fleet, which now proceeded towards the Italian coast. On board our ship was an ape, the property of the captain; and by the curious tricks of this animal we were greatly amused. An old gentleman of Naples was likewise on board, in the character of a passenger: he wore a perruque, and the ape had for a long time cast wistful glances thereon: his intentions were obviously to abstract it, but they were foiled by the watchful diligence of the proprietor. One day, however, when we had just passed the Stromboli, and every one's attention was absorbed by the view of Etna, which lay before us, the mischievous monkey took advantage of our reveries to spring upon the Neapolitan, to seize the unfortunate wig, and to bound, before any one could intercept him, up to the cross-stay of the middle-mast. The lamentations of the bereaved old gentleman, whose bald pate was thus left unprotected, excited, on the one hand, our universal commiseration; but, on the other, when we looked up at the ape, who had put on the perruque the wrong side foremost, we burst into involuntary shouts of laughter, which after a while infected the good-natured loser himself.

It was quite impossible to catch the thief, who climbed successively to the very highest point of the mast, making so many grimaces that we were fairly compelled to hold our sides. In the evening he descended, bearing with extreme carefulness the stolen perruque under his arm, and hastening to his crib, which was situated under the step of the cabin, where we secured him, and rescued the wig, which we restored to its disconcerted owner.

Nothing was safe from the depredations of this ill-natured animal: every thing that came in his way he purloined. He penetrated into the sleeping-rooms of the soldiers—seized the rum-bottles—took them away—thieved the caps—and retired with his booty into the masts, &c. &c. These gambols served to divert us infinitely; and as the length of the voyage was not such as to occasion tedium, we derived there-from both health and pleasure.

We had left the Sicilian coast in the beautiful season of May, when nature was invested with a robe of surpassing loveliness. The air was genial—the heavens pure and serene: thousands of fishes sported around our vessel, and innumerable sea-birds wheeled about the masts, ready to devour whatever might be thrown overboard. The ship had not to contend against any violence on the part of the waves, which uniformly greeted her starboard; and the crew were freed from the labour of making alterations in the tackle. At length, a calm held us enchained some days near the Liparian islands; but with a renewal of the same wind which had wafted us from Milazzo, we made further way. The mariners were kind and sociable; and cleanliness was unremittingly observed. We ourselves had no work whatever to do, and were abundantly supplied with food. In a word, every thing was joy and contentment.

CHAPTER 11

To England

Soon did we perceive in the blue distance the coast of Italy, and picturesque objects started into view almost every minute—the prospect undergoing perpetual change. But the proportion of our delight was greatly enlarged when a nearer approach to shore enabled us to see these things, which had been before blended in harmonious confusion by distance, in all their beauteous detail. The bay of Naples, backed by the town itself, stretched out in the shape of an amphitheatre, made a sublime impression upon our minds. On one side of the city towered Vesuvius, with its neighbour, the Monte Somme; the former always crowned with vapoury cloud, the latter covered well nigh to the summit with grapes, the juice of which often served us to drive away care and spleen. The whole country on both sides of the bay is, in fact, like one huge garden, in which bloom all the varieties of southern fruit. The line of the coast is thickly strewed with batteries, in the loop-holes of which are placed pieces of cannon of the largest calibre, looking as if they would oppose the advance of every passing ship. We, however, sailed quite peacefully into port, accompanied by innumerable boats and gondolas, filled with well-dressed ladies and gentlemen, who alternately raised the cry of King Ferdinand and King George. Every vessel in the harbour hoisted a flag, and we did the same. The press and crowd of people upon the shore can hardly be described. Elegant carriages, fiacres,—lazzaroni, chevaliers, ladies and gentlemen, soldiers of the now dissolved army of Murat,—all were swarming like bees together. The swell of the sea was at this time very strong, and therefore we were disabled from landing till next morning: however, we were pretty soon at anchor, but the rest of the day was spent rather tediously, as was also the ensuing night—everyone being possessed with an ardent longing to explore the interior of the beautiful town which lay before our eyes. Each man was desirous to render his arms and accoutrements as good-looking as possible, in order to attract the admiration of the Neapolitan people, who have a great fondness for display.

The wished-for dawn at length broke, and we disembarked without loss of time; the whole expedition, in the course of an hour, passing in review before the royal palace, in the gallery of which the entire staff of the troops then in Naples was assembled. Our corps was particularly distinguished in respect to its appearance, bearing, and attire; and it might clearly be read in our countenances that we had been well entertained whilst on board. In a word, all eyes were directed towards the new-comers, and expressions of pleasurable surprise were passed commonly from one to another, occasionally varied by curses of Murat and his party.

A good many of the Austrian troops whom we met here, presented, on the other hand, a most pitiful figure;—by reason partly of their white uniform, which, from its tendency to soil, is unfitted for military service; and partly owing to the victuals which had been furnished to them, in a shameful manner, by the commissioners. I myself frequently had occasion to observe that these poor fellows were fed upon bread consisting more of straw and bran-grudgeon than of corn. They complained also, in particular, of the heavy marches which they had made from the Po to Naples; and in addition to these evils, their pay was scandalously inadequate; they having received only two kreuzers a-piece daily, with the promise that their remaining money should be paid to them afterwards!

On the conclusion of the review, we were made acquainted with the situation of our quarters, which were fixed in the district of Santa Magdalena, in the back-ground of the bay, at the southern end, near the base of Vesuvius. I should have liked exceedingly to have made an excursion to the adjacent ruins of Pompeii and Herculaneum; but the soldiers of Murat, who were roaming about in lawless bands, rendered travelling very unsafe. We went however several times to Vesuvius without the permission of our officers, and intended to climb to its summit; but time was always wanting to enable us to do so: we were obliged therefore to satisfy ourselves with so much as we could see of the mountain without incurring punishment for our curiosity, returning generally much delighted. The fine prospects of the bay and city recompensed us fully for the fatigue of our various rambles.

King Ferdinand IV. speedily re-ascended his ancient throne, amidst the joyful acclamations of his subjects.[1] This circumstance gave occasion to a great many different festivities; and the Neapolitans exerted themselves by all the means in their power to exhibit their attachment to the restored monarch and his family.

Our business was now finished here; therefore we again embarked, and in the month of August, 1815, proceeded to Genoa, where we expected to receive our discharge, as had been decreed by the British parliament: this however was not even yet the case, and the spring of 1816 found us still in service.

We made the passage to Genoa in a very short period, being favoured both by wind and weather. Once more were my senses enchanted by the gulf of Naples and its beautiful environs,

---

1. King Ferdinand IV. of Naples, however much the popular ferment of the period alluded to might have reconciled his continental subjects to his restoration, was, beyond doubt, one of the most ineffective and truly despicable monarchs of Europe. He was in the habit of personally visiting the markets, and bargaining for meat and other provisions; and his life, altogether, was devoted to enjoyments of the most inferior and un-intellectual description,— eating and drinking, in particular. The inscription upon his statue in the Museum, denominated Gli Studij, begins as follows:— *"Ferdinando Bourbono Augusto, Xr. Religionis et Securitatis Publicæ Protectori Invicto:"*—notwithstanding which sounding exordium, however, it is pretty well known that this august and unconquered chieftain was obliged more than once to seek safety for his illustrious person in flight.

particularly by the gigantic volcano and the numerous vine-yards surrounding it, whose fruits had so often bewitched me in another sense: never shall I forget the exquisite flavour of the Lacryma Christi, which however I am doomed no more to taste. Our vessel glided pleasantly through the little narrow passes of Ischia and Procida, to both of which islands we approached near enough to distinguish the various objects on the land. At no great distance might be observed the crater of an extinguished volcano, and the shore was strewed with large and small pieces of pumice-stone. Lovely vineyards stretched themselves over the rest of each island, whilst oranges and other trees peculiar to the warm south were growing in large quantities.

By and by all this scene disappeared, and was succeeded by a view of the promontory on which Terracina is situated. Without experiencing any cross accident, we approached to Elba and to the adjoining island of Capraja, which latter rises quite bare out of the surface of ocean, like a huge sand-down. This island is in fact uninhabited, and is frequented only by dwellers in Liburna and Genoa, for the purpose of fishing.

Near the last-mentioned place, we observed the castle of Diamanti, which forms the highest summit of the fortifications of the town, and is only visible in clear weather; its guns commanding the whole port and roadstead. The lighthouse is the first object perceived on entering the harbour of Genoa, the approach to which is so narrow, that from either side the entrance of a vessel can be, if not wholly prevented, at least rendered extremely difficult. Close by is the place of public execution; mid just as our ship was passing, the gallows were graced by the exhibition of a long-bearded Genoese. On the old Mola we came to anchor, and so near shore, that without much effort we could spring to land. Here, in fact, we did disembark, and went, through the Punta del Banco, to the quarter St. Thomas.

Quite different did we find this part of Italy from its more southern regions: the habits of the people were more cleanly— their characters more refined and open; and it was easy to observe that we were by some degrees nearer to our dear native country.

Genoa, during its republican constitution, must have been a very considerable city; for on all sides we heard complaints of the diminution of commerce and prosperity; whilst, nevertheless, it appeared to us, that even at the present time both land and sea trades were going on very successfully. The many beautiful palaces, and other fine buildings, prove beyond doubt that the founders of Genoa must have been a wealthy and powerful people. The Doria Palace, at the Gate St. Thomas, as well as that near the Gate del Aqua, are certainly both very remarkable structures: in the latter was at that time lodging Major Gen. Phillips; and I had consequently frequent opportunities of seeing the inside of this fine edifice. Paintings in fresco, representing the wars of the Crusades, embellished the whole corridor, the lobbies, and antechambers; and often have I stood for hours together gazing on the athletic proportions and noble countenances of these heroes. The hall presented an arcade of several thousand led in length, on the walls of which were depicted groups of females weaving sails. A stranger would stand a chance of utterly losing his way by following the labyrinthine cross-ways of this huge apartment.

The galley-slaves in the naval arsenal demand a word or two of notice. These men are inured to the hardest labour; and often did I observe the poor wretches, who by the bye are composed of the most depraved and vilest of the population, dragging, like beasts of burden, loads of tremendous weight. The arsenal itself is very large, and contains all the warehouses which are concerned in the trade of ship-building: and it is a great pity that this port possesses only wharfs for small ships and galliots, which latter, however, are very useful, both to defend the coast and to make excursions in; often starting from the port to engage with the corsairs, who are continually crossing this part of the Mediterranean. Some days previously to my departure, for instance, a Tunisian corsair was captured by one of these small vessels.

The fortifications of Genoa are regular, and their construction has been attended with considerable expense. Mounting the walls at the Porta St. Thomas, you may walk without interruption all round the city, the parapet being built of brick, and kept in excellent repair.

The severity of the current winter tried us a great deal; as, from long experience of warmer climates, we found a northern aspect intolerable. Most of us indeed had not witnessed, for several years, either ice or snow in any degree deserving notice.

In the spring of 1816 we embarked for England, on the coast of which we arrived in the month of March: here I grew ill, and fell shortly afterwards into a nervous fever of long duration, which brought me nigh to death's door. I was conveyed to the military hospital at Portsmouth, where I lay for a considerable time quite senseless; my comrades meanwhile being honourably discharged, and sent home to their native countries—a fact which came to my knowledge at a subsequent period. Repeatedly did I, to all appearance, rapidly recover, and as often severe relapses threw me back into my former state of sickness; so that, after the expiration of a year and a half, I was still on English ground, and in the English service: at length I was so far restored as to render my discharge no longer ineligible. During my illness I had saved a little money, so that I might perhaps have been worth the sum of a hundred guldens.[2]

The day of my departure was fixed, when by chance I was introduced to the notice of an officer of high rank, who wanted a servant. I engaged myself to this gentleman at a monthly salary of four pounds; and for the space of a year and a half I continued perfectly satisfied. One source of my comfort may have been probably derived from my master's acquaintance with the habits of my own countrymen; for servants in England, speaking generally, are not kindly treated, being regarded by their employers more as necessary evils than in any other light.

After some time, my master was ordered from Portsmouth, to be incorporated into a regiment which was in garrison in the metropolis. It was with considerable regret that I found myself obliged to quit this sea-port, where I had formed many agreeable connexions, and had altogether passed my time very pleasantly.

2. A gulden is the eleventh part of a sovereign.

Portsmouth has so large a harbour, that it is capable, if necessary, of sheltering the whole English fleet, and is defended by three forts. The wharfs for ships and ammunition are quite astonishing, both as regards convenience and extent. A hospital and a naval school, each arranged for the reception of 3,000 persons, are admirably appropriate to the place. Almost every hour vessels arrive from the various parts of the world which are engaged in commerce. In every quarter of the town, you may hear different sorts of languages—including those of civilized Europe and the ruder tongues of Asia and America; native and foreign sailors thronging about in all directions, in search of the universal object—pleasure.

The inhabitants of the place, however, avoid as much as possible any connexion with these sons of Neptune, who, for the most part, are drunken and mischievous: at the same time, much kindness is shown to them when they are placed in circumstances which call for its exercise, as is not unfrequently the case. The guard-rooms are often filled with such guests; the sailors of English vessels not seldom gracing these receptacles, being much accustomed to be overcome by liquor, and having generally more money to spend than the seamen of other countries. When so thoroughly intoxicated as to be scarce able to raise an arm, they will challenge every person they meet,—shaking their double fists as if to level with the earth their supposed antagonists: hence the guards are obliged to fall upon them in a body, in order to secure them and to prevent mischief. When overpowered, and lying as it were in immoveable masses, they resort to the use of oaths, cursing God, and swearing at every body around: it then becomes necessary to gag them; which process is performed by putting a stick across the mouth, fixed by a string passed behind the hat—so that neither the lips nor tongue can be at all moved. Thus the swearing and roaring are prevented, and blubbering succeeds, only terminated by exhaustion and sleep.

Such is a specimen of the extravagance of these people, which pervades, in fact, all their actions;—and yet, in spite thereof, they are by the natives of this maritime country much more respected and humoured than men attached to the land service. I have myself, during my stay here, witnessed the infliction of gross insults by the lowest of the populace upon both officers and privates of the military, whilst the most shabby-looking sailors were treated with astonishing courtesy.

The soldier is, in truth, upon English ground, an undervalued being, distasteful to all ranks, except perhaps the very highest, by whom he is more regarded as an useful engine than with any sympathy in his pursuits or feelings. Throughout the whole kingdom, the barracks of the military are placed outside the towns, within which not even the commanding officers reside; the soldiers being only at stated intervals of the day permitted to enter the town, and being then frequently watched by the Sergeant. Under these circumstances, the English soldier feels himself more advantageously situated abroad than in his own country, and I was extremely happy that I was no longer attached to the standard of the British army.

I never could, indeed, from first to last, accustom myself to the English habits and manners; and I think that it almost amounts to an impossibility for any Frenchman or German to do so; for it is hardly to be described how proud, stiff, and reserved is the demeanour of the self-wrapped-up inhabitants of this island. Even those who have been travellers on the continent, and consequently necessitated, in some degree, to accustom themselves to the good German manners, are arrogant enough.

Chapter 12

London

Now I swam again upon the deceitful element, and in a vessel of a character quite novel to me—a steam-boat. Utterly surprised was I on entering this vessel, the ingenious arrangement of which powerfully excited my curiosity, seeing that it took the place at once of both sails and wind. That without either mast or canvass the boat should outstrip in speed the swiftest sailing-vessel, appeared to me at that time little less than miraculous. Thus whilst we fled along, the shores quickly receded; and in the course of this voyage I obtained a glimpse of Deal and Dover, two large coasting towns; opposite the latter of which, in the blue distance, lay Calais and the French shore;—so near was I to that land which contained my beloved family. A yearning of affection for my country and my friends came over me; but the desire of becoming better acquainted with the world,—so fair an opportunity of indulging which was now before me,—overcame every other feeling.

We anchored by Deal for a few hours, to set ashore passengers. Here is no port, only an open roadstead, which was filled with ships; and here, as well as at Portsmouth, were a great many dismantled men-of-war, their crews being discharged, and roaming about the different seaport towns, destitute of employ—the English naval force having undergone a great reduction since the peace with France.

Shortly afterwards we rounded the point of Dover, and hastened towards the mouth of the Thames, into which our vessel soon darted. Up the river we went with increased velocity, and but a short time elapsed before the giant-city,—the capital of all the capitals of Europe—rose upon our view. The mere sight of this vast wonder is sufficient almost to realize the English boast, that London alone is as large as all the principal towns of France united.

The river was filled with vessels of every size and description. An immense number of boats were sailing up and down— some with provisions —others with coals—others, again, with parties of pleasure merely. In a word, the whole presented the semblance rather of a huge public street than of a river. We soon arrived at the Custom-house; and although come from an English sea-port, my master was obliged to produce his papers, and I to exhibit his effects, in order to make manifest that there were amongst them no foreign articles subject to duty. My master being a military officer, was not long detained; and I hastened, as quickly as possible, with two porters, whose assistance I had engaged for ten shillings, to our lodgings, which were not very distant from the landing-place; so that my surprise was excited by their asking so much for such a little way: my master however did not think it exorbitant, and paid the money without hesitation.

The first impression made on my mind by the sight of this vast city was not altogether agreeable; and one principal cause of this may be found in the smoky atmosphere by which its long narrow streets are enveloped, and which clothes even the cupolas of its towers. As I approached it by the river, the fine country spread around relieved greatly this dusky hue, and formed a striking contrast, in its clearness and beauty, to the sombre mass before me. The capital is seven miles in length, and five miles in breadth, and is computed to contain about 150,000 houses, and a million of inhabitants.[1] The general material employed in building is brick, which soon assumes, owing to the universal use of sea-coal fires, a sooty appearance; and even where archi-

---

1. The author is pretty accurate in his account of the dimensions, &c. of our great metropolis.

tectural elegance has been displayed, the confined situation of such edifices renders it almost impossible to view them to advantage, if indeed they are not wholly overlooked. Most of the houses are two stories in height above the ground-floor; having an underground kitchen, with cellar and other appurtenances. The servants' apartments, generally speaking, are not at all to my taste, although my lodging was, it must be confessed, a little better. The streets have all of them flag-stones on each side, for the accommodation of foot-passengers, who would otherwise incur great hazard from the quantity of equestrians, and of carriages of every description.

The communication between the city and the borough of Southwark,[2] intercepted by the Thames, is rendered facile by means of five bridges, to which a sixth has just been added. Amongst these the two iron bridges are the most remarkable, which are about 1200 feet long and forty feet wide. The older ones are embellished with carved figures; but it struck me as not a little strange, that the banks of this noble stream, flowing as it does through the first commercial city in the world, should be destitute of quays and other ornamental structures, such as I have seen in Paris and elsewhere.

The shops and warehouses are so numerous and elegant as to baffle all description: they occupy the whole of the ground-floor; and, in this respect, London by far excels any other town. I was soon enabled to observe, that these places not only attracted the females of the metropolis to gaze at them, and to make purchases of various kinds, but were used by these fair ones as rendezvous for meetings with persons of the other sex,—a circumstance by no means objected to by the shopkeepers themselves.

In both winter and summer, this great city is beautifully lighted up with gas, the glare of which species of illumination seems to render unnecessary any assistance from the heavenly luminaries. I had no opportunity, during my stay, of seeing more than the outside of the several remarkable public buildings, with the exception of the Tower, whither my master, who

---

2. The author erroneously says Westminster.

had to transact business there, took me. This place might be with greater propriety called Towers, there being more than one, which serve to form the castle or fort, and protect the other buildings of the enclosure. I took only a slight view of these buildings, consisting of numerous streets, &c. The Tower Chapel was closed; but a soldier of the garrison, who was on duty, told me that many victims of despotism were buried here, and confirmed his assertion by naming certain instances. The menagerie contains a good many wild beasts; but they bore the appearance, to me, of being in a very sickly state. Although I should have been much gratified thereby, I could not obtain admission to view the jewels of the imperial crown. The armoury did not please me: it contains an immense quantity of arms, of every description—some amongst them being exceedingly curious; but I had little satisfaction in gazing upon these instruments of destruction. The Mint is likewise close in the neighbourhood, but I could not see its interior.

This was the sum total of what I saw in the Tower of London: there are many other spectacles exhibited therein; but the payment of a shilling for each sight rendered the amusements too dear for the pocket of a servant.[3]

---

3. The fact of payment being required at the entrance of our principal public metropolitan buildings,—so disgraceful in itself to our character as a nation, and particularly so as contrasted with our continental reputation for riches,—has been so often stated by foreigners, and so universally quoted with marks either of surprise or vituperation, that it may be said to form a standing topic in all foreign works in which the habits of our country are commented on. That it should be matter of astonishment and indignation to a Parisian—the inhabitant of a city in which all the wonders of ancient and modern art, the interiors of palaces, and the beauties of gardens (even royal gardens) are thrown open gratuitously to the public gaze and enjoyment;—that to him, we say, the pitiful and paltry price at which we sell our national credit in this way, and by which (not to speak it profanely) the sacred chapters of St. Paul and Westminster realise an unholy profit—should be the subject of ridicule and abuse,—is not so surprising; for Paris is rich, and can afford, as London can, to be liberal: but that such meanness and extortion should excite the evidently angry sneer of a native of Germany—a land in which tyranny has repressed all wealth but that of mind,—truly is, or ought to be, most humiliating to our national vanity.

The town-house, or Guildhall, of the city, seemed to me no larger than that of many German towns. The exterior is embellished with statues; and inside is an immense room, on entering which you are struck with the appearance of two gigantic figures rudely constructed of wood, and pitifully daubed with paint. These monsters are denominated Gog and Magog, and many grotesque stories are told of them by the lower classes. The hall is ornamented, besides, with numerous pictures and statues of royal and otherwise distinguished individuals.

The Exchange is a structure well worthy of observation, it being the very nucleus of commerce, where merchants of every nation under the sun congregate daily.

The Bank of England is of immense extent, and its exterior struck me as being remarkably handsome. The interior, with which I am unacquainted, is said to be not so good; but the importance of the establishment to the general interests of this mercantile kingdom is inconceivably great. The statue of Charles II. which ornaments one of the entrances, looks more like that of a Turk than of an Englishman.

Somerset House bears more of the appearance of a palace than any other public building in London, It is situated in the very heart of the capital, on the bank of the Thames, which is there wider than at any other point of its metropolitan channel: but you have no view of the river except at the back of the edifice; and even there, the prospect of the noble line of hills which rise on the opposite side is cooped in by wharfs and other buildings.

The first view of the splendid Gothic structure, called Westminster Abbey, filled me with admiration; a feeling which was not, however, increased upon a nearer scrutiny. The other churches of Westminster I did not examine, since they have no celebrity except on account of the monuments enclosed therein, which are valuable only to connoisseurs. St. Paul's Cathedral, with its two cupolas and magnificent dome, is venerable and imposing; but its interior strikes the beholder with nothing more than a sense of extent; the bare walls and vacant area producing an unfavourable contrast with the lavish richness of the external decoration.

The same observation which I made respecting the Westminster parish-churches will hold good with regard to those of the city, into which I felt no temptation whatever to enter.

The metropolis of Britain abounds with public charities of every kind, which have the reputation of being admirably adapted to their several purposes, and reflect peculiar honour upon the humane liberality by which they have been established.

The large coffee-houses, the Pantheon, and a number of other public buildings and walks, I saw only in passing; my small leisure and my master's short sojourn rendering any further acquaintance with them impossible. To each of the two great national theatres, Drury-Lane and Covent-Garden, I went but once: indeed, I had no occasion to repeat my visit in order to be convinced that they were not calculated to afford me the least gratification. The various other theatres I know by name alone.

Larger than in any other town in the world is the number of courtesans in London, who, like the greater part of their countrywomen, are extremely handsome, and who form separate classes amongst themselves;—independently of all which, a considerable body of married women and girls of fair reputation are to be met with, who bestow their favours with prudence and caution, keeping on the safe side of circumstances. The English females generally, however, are chaste and estimable, not enduring the least approach of voluptuousness either in word or deed; and it is very possible to forfeit their good graces altogether even by a single unguarded expression,—as was once the case in my own instance. I saw the daughter of a neighbour, whose trade was that of a farrier, in the act of sewing shirts, and asked her, without the most distant idea of giving offence, if she could recommend somebody who would do a similar good office for me. To this question, put in the greatest simplicity, I not only received no answer, but the girl's frowning countenance manifested that I had incurred her displeasure. I was afterwards informed by a friend, that the custom of the country forbade any allusion, in the presence of virtuous females, to shirts, chemises, garters, small-clothes, or any other article worn in the immediate vicinity of the person. The women of the lower classes, however, are treated by their husbands with great coarseness and vulgarity, against the exercise of which they do not even venture to remonstrate. It is said that instances occasionally occur of wives being sold by their spouses in the public market, but nothing of the kind took place during my stay; and I am disposed to regard the circumstance, if it ever does happen, as one equally rare as disgusting.

The salutations in use amongst these haughty islanders are altogether different from those which custom has established amongst the Germans. Frequently have I heard a fine gentleman commence his address to an acquaintance thus:"D—n you, you dog! how d'ye do?" or, "Where the devil did you come from?" nor are the other parts of their colloquy free from the introduction of similar refinements. When in the company of ladies, however, this mode of talking is wholly laid aside, and they become, for the most part, reserved and silent: indeed, the minutes seem to be anxiously counted until the retirement of the females enables them to indulge in those parts of speech native to and beloved by them.

I had heard that it was considered fashionable in London to be out of health at certain periods of the year: my little circle was perhaps too humble to adopt this mode; but there was no lack of sickness nevertheless. Nervous disorders are a good deal patronised by the Londoners, at least by the upper classes amongst them; but cases of this kind did not fall within my observation. I hope the temperate habits and disposition to labour so common in Germany, will prevent my countrymen from falling victims to this English malady.

Instances of self-destruction were reported to me almost daily, and the reasons assigned for them often excited my surprise; whilst the English, on the contrary, thought them quite sufficing. The epitaphs on the grave-stones, in the various burial-places, struck me as being frequently very strange: as, for instance, I read in one place,—"My wife has turned me out of the world: death has become my life, and the king of terrors my brother."

A true and thorough description of the English character would probably be beyond my ability: I feel indeed that much higher talents than my own are requisite to comprehend and set down its subtle peculiarities. Frequently when I believed that I had made up my mind on the subject, fresh circumstances induced me to alter my opinion, and a new aspect of the national character was presented to my mind. Often did I feel acutely my want of the address and general intelligence necessary to enable a man to mix with confidence in the society of this wondrous place; where even the depraved portion of its inhabitants—the common thieves—carry on their profession with a tact and skill, that require, in order to counteract them, the exercise of unwearied caution. Social life in London, particularly amongst the polished circles of the west end, differs essentially in its peculiarities from the methods adopted in Germany. When we retire to rest, the fashionables of the British metropolis begin to congregate for pleasure; and at the pale dawn, universal bustle and animation still continue. At three o'clock p. m. the Bond-street lounger, just turned out, salutes his friend with "good morning!" and after dinner, which is taken at seven or eight o'clock, or perhaps later, he exchanges this phrase for "good evening!" so that for him there is no noon at all. These dinners last sometimes, at least the wine and dessert, until the very middle of the night, by which means supper becomes superfluous, tea being served directly after dinner. During the meal, little is said, and no great deal of wine drunk, all continuing pretty orderly: but no sooner is the cloth removed, which is a mute sign for the retirement of the ladies, than strong wines are set upon table, and lustily pushed about. With the circulation of the glass politics are introduced, and often canvassed with no small asperity; seldom one of the guests departing without having paid due homage to the rosy god Bacchus, even to the extent, in some instances, of prostration under the table.

Very different from this, however, are the proceedings of the plebeian classes. From the earliest to the latest hour, these people are in constant activity. At break of dawn, numerous carts and other conveyances are on the alert for the supply of the metropolis with various articles of food, such as vegetables, &c. which are brought in cart-loads from the surrounding country places. Later in the morning are to be seen numbers of coal-drays, drawn by gigantic black horses, the motion of which to and from the coal depôts is well nigh perpetual, and by which all parts of the town are supplied. As the day advances, the carriages and cabriolets are put into activity, between which it is sometimes difficult for the pedestrian to steer with safety across the road. Men with bills stuck upon their hats, or at their backs, go about the streets, offering, for some penny or so, their printed songs, lists of malefactors, dying speeches, &c. or forming a kind of locomotive advertisement to some trading establishment. Thus the scene eternally changes throughout the whole capital; and on the approach of evening the crowds even increase, owing to numbers of the working-people getting free from their day's business—nor is quiet restored until midnight, and then only partially.

What a contrast to this ever-active principle of life and motion is presented by the dull, stagnant, unendurable monotony of the Sunday! It affords certainly a remission of labour to the mechanic who toils through all the rest of the week; but to the man of fashion, in particular, its stupidity must be tedious in the extreme. All mirthful indulgences, whether public or private, are strictly forbidden; and before the termination of the day even those who had been longing for it during all the previous six, seem heartily tired of their holiday.

My short residence in London, and the super-added want of time and opportunity, prevented me from obtaining more than a superficial knowledge of its various characteristics; and there are already so many acute and interesting accounts of the British metropolis furnished by men of talent, that the limited nature of my information is scarcely matter of regret.

Chapter 13

The East Indiaman

In the spring of the year 1818 I accompanied my master on a journey to Gravesend, at which place he visited his friend Captain Dalrymple, of the East-India Company's naval force: I acquired the favourable notice of this latter gentleman, and was by him persuaded to go in his service on a voyage to China. In the vessel I became acquainted with a young German, who then filled the office of midshipman; and I will take advantage of his journal to make my readers informed of the particulars of our voyage, adding such circumstances as occurred to myself individually.

On the morning of the 14th of April, 1818, the *Cabalva*, an East-Indiaman, of about 1,200 tons, destined by the direction of the Honourable Company for the coast of China, and commanded by Captain Dalrymple, set sail from Gravesend. The ship's company consisted altogether of 130 men; including six officers, a surgeon, an assistant-surgeon, seven midshipmen, one passenger, who had been a purser in the employ of the Company and was destined for Canton, and the servant of the captain. At Gravesend I [1] went on board as midshipman; and the captain, who behaved very kindly to me, as I had made the same voyage with him once before, offered me, in proof of his friendship, the vacant situation of sixth officer. In the commencement, I was unwilling to undertake this charge, which was attended with

---

1. The reader will please to observe, that it is the author's friend who speaks, during this narrative, in the first person.

few solid advantages and would entail upon me some expense: but the captain succeeded in repressing these objections, and accordingly the coat-sleeve of my uniform became decorated with six buttons.

We endeavoured to make our crew as complete as possible, and having done so, set sail in company with the *Lady Melville*, a vessel like-wise in the Honourable Company's service. We passed through the Channel under a favourable wind but in dusky weather, being guided by an old experienced pilot. At eleven o'clock in the forenoon of the 17th instant, whilst proceeding quietly under easy sail, and making eleven knots an hour (the Ower-light ship being N. N. E. of us), we in one instant found ourselves aground—at first slightly, but subsequently experiencing, four or five times, very powerful concussions. Our pilot, alarmed by this sudden and unforeseen mishap, grew pale, but shortly recovering his self-possession, he directed the helm to be put a-port, and we again got sea-room and resumed our voyage. The ship-carpenter was instructed to examine the vessel, and reported that there was four inches water in the well, which in a very short period increased to nine inches. A council was now held, to decide whether we should proceed, or go into port to get our ship caulked. The decision was to proceed; and the pilot, quite dejected in consequence of this misfortune, having been put ashore, we again made way.

By the leak the water increased fourteen inches an hour, and we were compelled to set the pumps in motion, and to work at them day and night. Both wind and weather however were in our favour; and we should have been perfectly contented, did not the unceasing noise of the pumps, and the staggering of the ship at the least sea that struck her constantly remind us of our danger.

We passed, with the customary ceremonies, the equinoctial line; and shortly afterwards there arose amongst our people a formidable revolt, which would have been attended with very mischievous consequences, had not the resolute conduct of the captain and officers speedily repressed it.—Captain Dalrymple dined one day on board the *Lady Melville*, which was always in our close company. The officer who commanded in his absence was desirous of exhibiting to him the skill of our seamen in reefing and handing; and accordingly turned out the hands to reef topsails, promising to each a glass of grog, in case it was done well. Unluckily those who were on the fore-top executed their task in such a bungling manner, that the fore-topsail was absolutely spoiled; in consequence of which they were immediately ordered down, and severely started. A good deal of grumbling and discontent hence ensued amongst the crew, several of whom stood daringly forth, and did not hesitate to use very menacing expressions. These were promptly imprisoned—a circumstance which, far from tranquillizing, served still more to exasperate the crew; and when the captain, at eight o'clock in the evening, came aboard, the hands were turned out for punishment. The lanterns were instantly lighted, and one of the culprits seized up: the boatswain was ready to execute the captain's sentence, so soon as it should be pronounced; when, at once, as on a given signal, a number of belaying-pins, (short iron bolts,) which seemed to be thrown from the masts, came rattling upon the heads of the officers and those who remained faithful to their duty; and with a furious "hurra" the whole gang rushed on us, shouting "Now all for one, and one for all!" with other expressions of defiance. "Hand up the arms!" vociferated the captain: and in a few moments each of us was provided with pistol, sword, &c. In the mean time the captain had directed that the shrouds should be searched, to discover, if possible, the perpetrators of the outrage. I, together with the second officer, performed this duty. We inspected every corner with the points of our swords, but could perceive no one. My companion descended again upon deck, having instructed me to stay in the main-top. The punishment of the condemned sailor now proceeded without further disturbance, and he received four dozen lashes; bat scarcely had the second culprit been seized up in like manner, when a great confusion arose again amongst the crew, and another storm of iron bolts was hurled upon the officers. The captain cried out to me that there must be some miscreant concealed aloft, but I assured him it was not the case; and at that instant a fellow was detected upon deck, in the very act of heaving the offensive missiles, and who, without the least delay, was visited with six dozen lashes. In a similar manner five others were punished, each being admonished to be cautious how he misbehaved in future, and to attend to his duty; and the affair being brought to an end, the crew were dismissed, but not without manifesting a good deal of dissatisfaction. No confidence was therefore placed in them by the officers, who continued the whole night under arms;—but all remained quiet.

We proceeded on our voyage with a favourable wind; and, at the Cape of Good Hope, fell in with the Honourable Company's ship the *Scalesby Castle*. From this vessel we learnt that the Ower-light ship, just before we crossed the Channel, had drifted several miles in shore; by which intelligence the enigma was solved of our having run aground in such well-known roads; and the pilot, captain, and indeed the whole ship's company, were cleared of any neglect or ignorance on the subject. We now perceived that it must have been the elbow-point of the Owers, a well-known reef near Portsmouth, on which we were so suddenly stranded, seduced by the false situation of the light-ship. By the same channel, our captain received the pleasant intelligence that his wife had been safely delivered of a little girl.

Some days after, we were separated, in a gale, from the *Scalesby Castle* and the *Lady Melville*; and our leak grew larger and larger, so that we had twenty inches water every hour. Under these circumstances, we agreed not to proceed directly for China, but to anchor at Bombay for the purpose of caulking the ship. A contrary wind did not permit us to sail directly up the channel of Mozambique; therefore we took the outer passage, intending to steer between the isles of St. Mauritius, or Isle de Franco, and Bourbon. The hands at the pumps were doubled, and the officers were commanded not to carry too much sail, lest the ship should be strained, and the leak increase.

Wind and weather had continued favourable ever since we rounded the Cape; and on Sunday, the fifth of July, we believed ourselves to be in the vicinity of St. Mauritius, where the captain had a brother who was colonel in the army, and whom he was desirous to see on the present opportunity. The whole of this day and subsequent night, therefore, we were engaged in endeavouring to discover land; but the weather was hazy and rainy, and the dawn of the next morning arose, without unfolding to us the least sign of it.

On Tuesday the seventh of July, at four o'clock a. m., on the watch being relieved as usual, and myself called upon deck to take the morning watch, under command of the second officer, I was instructed to keep a good lookout ahead, as our course began to appear dubious. Having therefore relieved the fourth officer, I stationed two men on the fore-yard, and one on each cat-head, mustered the forecastle watch, and walked the waist, in expectation of receiving orders for washing the deck.

The moon had already disappeared about an hour, and it wanted pretty much the same time to daybreak: the night was at its very darkest, but the sky was cloudless and the stars bright,— the wind was brisk but not heavy,—and the *Cabalva* cut her way majestically through the dusky waves: we made seven miles and a half an hour, going under easy sail, with a breeze on the quarter. The crew were for the most part stretched in sleep upon the decks, and the heavy melancholy stillness was only interrupted by the sea breaking against our bows, the snoring of the sailors, and the measured steps of the officers—diversified occasionally by the doleful cry of the birds flying above our masts.

Thus I had paced up and down perhaps half an hour, looking now upwards, now around me,—one moment at the sparkling stars—the next at the black horizon, where sea and sky were blended in one line,—anxious to perceive any impending danger, yet little thinking that it was even now upon us,—when suddenly the men stationed aloft shouted out repeatedly, one after another, "Breakers—breakers on the larboard-bow! hard a-port! hard a-port! Too late! All is lost! hard a-port!"

My faculties were perfectly benumbed by these exclamations; and I felt for the moment as if enchained by heart-withering ice; but I had sense enough to be aware that there was not a single instant to lose, I echoed the ominous words to the other officer of the watch, and ran quickly aft to the wheel: the helm flew aport, the vessel rounded to, glanced for a few seconds over the rocky bottom, and then, with a tremendous hurl, she struck. By the violence of the concussion, her bottom was entirely quashed; the masts trembled like aspens; and every thing was crackling and bursting around. The wheel spun round like a top, until the helm was hard a-starboard again; by which action the man at the wheel was cast clean over to leeward, where he lay, the picture of death. I saw him no more: probably he was actually killed on the spot, or so mutilated as to be unable to seek his own preservation. One of the seamen whom I had placed on the fore yard-arm was likewise thrown down, and was either dashed to pieces or carried away by the waves.

All hands now assembled upon deck—the final concussion having cast most of the sailors out of their hammocks and cots, and no one being willing to remain between decks. Thus, in a few moments, the upper deck was thronged with half-naked people, and a horrible scene of confusion, dismay, and uproar, was exhibited before us;—the orders of the captain and other officers being almost drowned in the prevailing tumult, which was aided by the splitting of the masts, the riving of the sails, and the bursting of the ribs of the vessel—the sea meanwhile driving over us, sometimes to the height of fifteen feet. On all sides the cry arose of "Loosen the boats—set them afloat:" this, however, was easier said than done, since all joined in the exclamation, but no one put his shoulder to the work, and the vessel heeled so violently from side to side, that it was well nigh impossible to set foot firmly upon her.

"Cut away the mainmast! down with the foremast! stand clear the masts!" was often shouted. Every one got out of the way as fast as he could, in order to avoid the hazard of the falling timbers; and a dreadful silence of some minutes duration ensued, during which the work was accomplished with hatchets and similar instruments, until the masts gave way, and fell with all their tackling into the foaming ocean.

"There goes the *Cabalva*!" said I to myself, with an irrepressible pang: still I did not abandon all hope, and redoubled my efforts to protract her utter destruction, by assisting to throw overboard the anchors, bowsprit, and whatever else might lighten the vessel; the braver amongst the sailors helping us with the good-will of man towards man: as for obedience and subordination, they had become idle words, to which no meaning was attached.—No sooner are the masts cut away in a sinking ship, than the feeling of perfect equality arises amongst her crew.

CHAPTER 14

Shipwreck

Morning dawned, and from the East the glorious sun up-rose, as if to mock our extremity. "Horror! horror! horror!" burst from the blanched and parched lips of the mariners, when daylight discovered the utter forlornness of our situation. It seemed to us, after a while, that we descried a sail in the distance, and this belief animated us with new courage: but when the sun had risen a little higher, we perceived that we were in error, having taken the grey point of a coral-reef for a ship. We worked meantime with almost supernatural effort, and in the very lap of danger, for the purpose of floating the large cutter, in which we at length succeeded, and some of the youngest and most active entered therein with eager precipitation, taking advantage of their superior strength to push aside sundry weak and invalid wretches, who were thereby left to shift for themselves. Capt. Dalrymple declined going off in this boat; but the sworn officers (at least the men who had been so called,) all jumped on board her, except the second, who afterwards reached shore by swimming in a cork jacket; as did likewise the surgeon, the purser, the passenger, some of the midshipmen, and several of the sea-men;—and the boat made directly for the reef.

Wearied to the last degree, I crept to the forecastle, wound my arms round the best bower anchor-stock, and looked earnestly out to see if I could discover either land, a sail, or any other consolatory object; but nothing calculated to give me comfort was visible; the dreadful coral-reef, and, further down, some low sand-banks, alone staring me in the face. After the space of an hour, the vessel burst asunder, the poop and forecastle alone remaining above water, and the furious breakers continually washing over these likewise.

Captain Dalrymple and some others were swimming amongst the ruins of the unfortunate *Cabalva*, hemmed round by pieces of mast, by yards, ribs, and spars—every moment covered by the waves. The large cutter, with thirty men, or thereabouts, who had sought her protection, was seen dancing upon ocean with miraculous adaptation to the humours of the angry element, until she touched the rock, when a tremendous surf broke over her with gigantic power, threw every soul clean out, and dashed them against the rocks: indeed, she would in all probability have turned broadside to the surf before, and been swamped with all the party, as they had no oars, had not one of the midshipmen used the precaution to make fast a rope to the wreck before they shoved off, the slack of which he eased out of the boat, as she was driven along by the waves, thus keeping her end on to the reef.

After a short interval, I descried the assistant-surgeon, an amiable young man, and one of my best friends, striking away from the wreck with infinite presence of mind. Unfortunately, however, he placed too much confidence in his swimming, and finally, after having nobly combated with many gigantic breakers, he sunk before my eyes into the boiling and self-tortured abyss.

Whilst I thus hung trembling upon the verge of eternity, but still clinging to a hope that I might reach the rock, about one hundred and fifty yards distant, my eyes gazing vacantly upon the mountains of water which came slowly rolling on, one overtopped by the other, and menacing with their snowy crests immediate destruction,—whilst the instinct of self-preservation constrained me to hold firmly on the wreck;—suddenly there stalked forth, and hobbled to me along some spars and pieces of wreck, from the cuddy, which was not quite under water, an old seaman; his eyes plainly proclaiming that he had employed the recent moments in spiritual exercise, in the captain's cabin. "I think, my dear sir," hiccuped he, "that it is now high time to be off out of this: a'nt you of the same opinion?"

"I don't know, Jones," answered I, "what advice it is best to give you; but, for my own part, I had rather weather it out here awhile longer."

"At any rate," rejoined Jones, "I must, upon my soul, get a quid of baccy: I can't do no longer without it;" and down he dives into the gun-deck, a small part of which was then standing out of water: he soon, however, emerges, holding the desired quid between his lingers, but quickly transferring it from them to his mouth. "Now, my dear sir," resumed he, "here I goes!" with which words he jumped gaily overboard, and actually succeeded in swimming to the rock. Although engaged in a ghastly struggle between life and death, I really could not forbear laughing when I looked after this true specimen of the English jack-tar. By good fortune, he caught hold, during his bathe, of a bale of cloth, by aid of which he steered along, and kept his body from being dashed against the rocks.

Those who, like myself, had still clung to different portions of the wreck, now grew every moment less in number. Some of them were already drowned: others had betaken themselves to a conflict with the billows: others again were drifting upon loose spars and rafts towards the reef: no assistance could possibly be rendered by one man to another. The eighty or ninety who had been left behind on the departure of the boat were now reduced to the number of about thirty, and these were in the most forlorn condition. Amongst them, I recognised the captain in his pea jacket and flannel dress, the fifth mate, and some midshipmen. This remnant was in the greatest possible embarrassment as to what course it was best to pursue; in which state of incertitude, they exhausted themselves to no effect; and a curious contrast to their exertions was visible in the conduct of certain sailors, who, like our friend before mentioned, were sitting in the captain's cabin, and drinking in courage under the semblance of champagne and brandy.

In the mean time, the long-boat, which was large enough to contain all the individuals now left behind, got clear of the wreck:

the captain, the fifth mate, myself, and about twenty sailors, took to it; but scarcely was she shoved off, before she went to pieces, being struck against some large planks, and every one was left to provide for his own safety as well as he could, several being drowned in the attempt. Capt. Dalrymple had stepped into the boat without saying a word, but his wild looks expressed clearly the anguish of his heart, and his condition was altogether truly pitiable. Not far from him, at the time of the boat's being stove in, was a poor lad, the servant of our mess, who was making his first voyage, and now sat covered with water. The fall of the timbers had broken his arm. He wept bitterly, and called aloud to me for assistance. My feelings were strongly excited: but what could I do? I was compelled to trust him to his own fortune, and shortly afterwards the waves took him away.

Soon after I had an opportunity of seeking safety on a large raft of booms, which was now breaking adrift from the wreck; and was enabled to pick up several fellow-sufferers by heaving a rope's end to them to lay hold of. The captain, with some difficulty, crawled from the mainmast to this raft, he having taken refuge upon the former after the destruction of the long-boat. I had sprung on the raft from the forecastle; and two midshipmen, with some twenty sailors, likewise contrived in various ways to gain it.

We were fairly launched, and drove towards the rock; but, as if fate would never weary of persecuting us, the spars turn broadside to the surf, by which they are so violently hurled about, that we are cast from one side to the other, and almost wholly incapacitated from holding on. When I bethink me of the actually miraculous manner in which I was preserved through this scene, my heart overflows with gratitude to my Creator. Many broke their arms and legs; and every individual striving to keep uppermost, the stronger trampled inhumanly upon the heads and shoulders of their feebler fellow-sufferers. It is impossible, however, to give other than a faint sketch of the scene to those who did not witness it. For my own part, at the approach of each breaker, I let go the spars, and betook myself to swimming until it had past—then grasping at them again. Having thus encountered twelve or fourteen of these formidable antagonists, the float was thrown upon the reef. Capt. Dalrymple, on whom I kept an eye as long as it was in my power, disappeared on the attack of the second breaker, and I saw him no more. Now that sorrow had removed all former animosity, his loss was universally lamented both by officers and men, since his behaviour had been at once kind and resolute, and marked by generous feelings towards every one. Six or seven seamen met their fate at the same time.

At length, worn out with toil and despair, we gained the rock, against which our frail conveyance was dashed with violence, and where we found our messmates plunged in the extremity of dismay, howling and lamenting instead of making any exertion to better their circumstances. Thus had we arrived on shore, if that name might be given to a piece of rock not many feet in length, and upon which we stood up to our middle in water.

However, my life was for the moment saved. My body was become, from the violence it had sustained, quite black and blue, and the whole of my clothing had been cut into shreds. My companions in suffering received me with a hearty welcome, and one man in particular professed his readiness to do me any service,—a circumstance which I shall never forget. No sooner had I arrived, than he gave me a glass of beer, and covered me with whatever he could procure for the purpose. This good friend's name was William Madden, and we had already, before this voyage, been messmates on board the *Marquis of Ely.*

Now arrived the captain's cutter, with the fifth officer, and five or six sailors, whom we had left on the wreck: the members of our forlorn party dispersed themselves on different points of the reef; and after a short interval, several corpses were washed ashore. We found that the number of drowned persons amounted to seventeen, including the captain and assistant-surgeon. All the officers and midshipmen, the purser, surgeon, passenger, and 110 sailors, were saved; but who could speculate on the continuance of this mercy? Escaping a watery grave, starvation stared us in the face.

Our situation was of a nature to battle all description, and could it have been observed by an uninterested spectator, must have presented a curious aspect. Our coral-reef, which was almost completely covered with water at the time we struck, but which, as the tide ebbed, rose gradually out of the sea, keeping off the vehemence of the surf,—was strewn all over with a confused heap of articles—the relics of the costly lading of the Cabalva; and might have worn the appearance of an enchanted island. Casks of wine, of beer, and brandy;—trunks and bales, some full, some empty;—gold, silver, steel, and glass, wrought in numberless shapes;—fine English muslin, Irish linen, &c.—all were mingled together in the greatest confusion.

Disorder, in fact, reigned not only amongst our rescued property, but, worst evil! amongst ourselves. The seamen, almost frantic, grew brutally selfish,—sacrificing to that all other feelings, and thus augmenting by ungenerous conduct the horrors of shipwreck. They betook themselves, in reckless style, to the wine and other stimulating liquids; cut open the bales of linen, and invested themselves therewith:—ship-boys, servants, the cook, and common sailors, were dressed in purple and scarlet robes, wearing white turbans, and strutting about like kings; whilst a great many sought insane satisfaction in destroying whatever came in their way.

Meanwhile the officers, in their miserable rags, were running here and there, and endeavouring, by every means in their power, to put a stop to these wanton outrages. Some of them knocked in the heads of the spirit and wine casks; some directed the building of a raft, and the repairing of the boats; whilst a few seamen wandered towards some low sand-banks, which lay three or four miles to the north-west. In the midst of all this confusion, and whilst some of the people were employed in swimming ashore, the gunner, an old Scotchman, immediately after having saved himself on the rock, seeing the guns tumble overboard, and take along with them large pieces of timber to which they were lashed, which said lashings belonged to his department,—made a cool observation to one of his mates, and received as cool a reply: "Ah, David!" says he, "our guns hold on well."

"Yes, sir," rejoined the other; "good lashings!"

I was sorry to observe that nothing was in the way of being steadily arranged for the general welfare. Had our boats been made thoroughly sea-proof, they could not, it is true, have contained half our number; but not even a single effort was perseveringly made, either with regard to them or to the construction of rafts; and meantime the water gradually rose, and we were fearful that the tide might come in the night and wash us away. After a while I strolled to the sand-banks, where indeed no great accession of safety could be expected, they being merely downs elevated some two or three feet above the surface of the sea, and subject to overflowing from the first tide. In spite of these dangers, however, I felt incited to make the trial, and proceeded thither in company with five or six sailors, each man taking with him a bottle or two of port, which, together with spirits, were in abundance upon our rock; but we were in want of fresh water, and eatables were out of the question.

Without shoes, and wading up to the hips in water, we struggled slowly over the hard and irregular shore, and were fortunate enough to meet with a young shark, which, after the lapse of half an hour, we killed, and haled him with a string to the bank. This timely supply promised us the materials of a dinner for fifteen or twenty men.

About noon, we reached a little sand-bank, which was not many feet above the surface of the sea: its length was about one hundred and forty yards, and its breadth about eighty. We found here a part of our people, and by and by arrived others; appearing, for the greater part, in the most grotesque and ridiculous garbs; and some carrying under their arms several bottles of wine, of which already they had taken no inconsiderable portion. Some were wrapped in pieces of cloth of the most glaring and brilliant colours—some in muslins and silks; most of them wearing, as before mentioned, a sort of turban; whilst a few had bonnets or fancy caps, which had been sent out to China as private trade: all had muslin, cloth, or beautiful skins wrapped round their feet, on account of their being very much lacerated while wading, like ourselves, from the wreck to the land, bare-footed; for not a single pair of shoes had we been able to save: all were provided with a decent stock of cherry brandy or wine, and of course pretty far gone. Some were asleep when we arrived, and a few employed in bandying jokes; whilst there were not wanting those who sought the dissipation of severer thought in quarrelling and boxing: some were sitting about, catching birds; which animals seemed perfectly astonished at our arrival, gazing on us with great curiosity, and approaching without the least consciousness of danger.

CHAPTER 15

Cast Ashore

I spoke with some sailors, who appeared the most prudent and courageous, to persuade them to return with me to the wreck; as I believed that, from the restoration of calm, it might be possible to save some victuals and water-casks before the ship went totally to pieces; but they answered me in such fine and elegant terms, and made such long harangues and speeches, that I soon gave over the task, convinced there was not a sober man amongst them. The large cutter had been hauled twenty or thirty yards upon the rocks soon after we had reached them; and the fifth officer, with eight men, after our departure for the sand, had moved her still more out of the way of the breakers, and, as we found afterwards, passed the night in her a little distance from the wreck.

A young man, who, had filled the office of captain's clerk, besought me, in imploring accents, to lie down by his side and die with him. I was by no means unwilling to gratify him in the former respect, since he had chosen for his exit a very comfortable spot; and I, tired out and bruised all over, and hopeless at the same time of the co-operation of my fellow-sufferers, was extremely desirous of rest; but with regard to the latter clause, I reserved that for further consideration. Shortly, a deep slumber fell over me; and when, after some hours, I awoke, I perceived the whole remainder of the ship's company assembled. Those who had last arrived, had brought with them from the wreck six or seven pieces of pork, three casks of fresh water, and some dozen bottles of wine; but altogether, even with the assistance of the shark and two or three lobsters, there was but a very spare dinner for 120 men.

In the afternoon, came the tide; and it set in so strong, that the rock was completely inundated, and the wind drove every thing light and floatable over towards our sand-bank, which was situated three or four miles to leeward of the wreck. We employed ourselves in seizing hold of every thing which appeared likely to be in any degree serviceable; but of this character we found but little, bearing indeed no proportion to the quantity of useless matters,—as for instance, essences and soaps—clothes and shoe-brushes—pomatum—books—hair and toothbrushes, muslin, &c. A very fortunate windfall occurred to us, however, after a while, and a universal cry of joy was lifted thereat on all sides:—it was a powder-cask, quite dry. With a razor and a piece of glass we struck a light; and, by the help of our newly-found powder, and some remnants of linen and other stuffs, we had shortly a comfortable fire.

Towards evening, we constructed a tent out of pieces of wood which had floated from the wreck, and covered it with fine English linen: in this, however, scarcely more than from forty to fifty men could find room. When it was completed and arranged as an asylum for the night as snugly as possible, by the exertions of the most active and skilful of our number—the ship-boys, cooks, sweepers, and other equally respectable members of the party rushed into it en masse, thus excluding the officers, to whom were left the honour and satisfaction of remaining unsheltered the whole night, exposed to rain and frost, as guards, heaven save the mark! of their worshipful comrades.

The apprehension which, until now, we had all along entertained, of being devoured by the waves, disappeared in the course of the night, when we were enabled to observe that the water was decreasing without having attained the height our fears had anticipated. Hence, although wet through with rain, and stiffened with frost, we saluted the rising day with renewed courage, and almost lively hearts. The refreshment of a night's sleep had restored their senses to a part of our crew. The small remainder of the provisions was, by general agreement of the well-disposed amongst us, placed under the eye and responsibility of the officers, in order to be divided fairly and properly. Still however there were many who stuck to the old motto of "every one for himself;" and these misguided men, stronger in number than the other party, engaged themselves in eating and drinking from morning to night, and would have corrupted the rest, had not the vigilance of the more prudent prevented it. It was a matter of great good luck, that the leaders of this faction resolved ultimately to separate from us, and construct on the other side of the bank (whither they imagined a good many casks of liquor had been drifted) a tent of their own. There they formed quite a distinct settlement, which very properly received the denomination of "Beer-Island."

As we had but a very scanty meal the day before, an early breakfast was served out on the morning of Wednesday, July the 8th, consisting of a small slice of fat pork about two ounces weight, and a dram of beer in a coffee-cup: neither biscuit, flour, or any vegetable substance, was to be found. It was resolved that we should pass this day to as good purpose as possible, with which object an arrangement was proposed to divide ourselves into different parties. Some of the strongest and bravest individuals amongst us offered of themselves to wade to the wreck in search of victuals and fresh water, the forecastle and poop being still visible between the breakers: to secure the large cutter was likewise an important object of this troop.

Another division went to the adjoining sand-banks, on which casks, bales, and other articles of lading of the *Cabalva* had floated. Those who were either feeble, sick, or indolent, (many belonging to the latter class from whom we had a right to expect better behaviour) remained still at home, as did likewise some working people, who erected a flag-pole, enlarged the tent, and unrolled bales of cloth, to dry them in the sun against night. Some, who would not submit to the general arrangement and discipline, were running disorderly about in all directions, without any particular object in view.

Mr. Sewell, the first officer, and I, were at the head of the party who went to the wreck. We departed a little while previous to low water, in order that we might be enabled to return some time before flood. After having waded two hours over a hard and rocky ground, up to our middle in water, we fell in with the large cutter, having on board the people who had been left behind yesterday, amongst whom we could soon perceive that some secret plan was in agitation, the completion of which, as it turned out, would have involved us in utter ruin. These men had commenced operations very quietly; but no long time had elapsed after our falling in with them, before they became rude and arrogant, directing their offensive language principally against the chief officer, and menacing us in we should attempt to take any thing out of the boat. When they became aware of our superior number, however, they struck a flag which they had hoisted, and one of them made us acquainted with the whole conspiracy.

These pretty fellows had purposed to abstract the boat, and to put out to sea on the noon of the same day, without sails, without rudder, without compass, and without any system of action or plan of navigation whatever. They must certainly have perished within the first day or two; and meanwhile the largest boat, we possessed,—in which, in fact, lay our only hope of eventual succour,—could never have been restored to us. We found the vessel laden with arms, cutlery, oars, watches, Spanish dollars, wine, brandy, beer, muslin, cloth, a drowned lamb, twelve drowned fowls, and a pine cheese, all heaped one upon another in precious confusion; and in the middle of the whole lay a certain good friend, who had wound six or seven large pieces of muslin around his left leg, which was thereby rendered as thick as his whole body. This man, on observing us, immediately, with the tone and language of a great sufferer, complained of his bad leg. "It is either broken or out of joint," said he, "and I have been in a great fever all the night, to allay which I could get nothing but brandy and port: I can exist no longer." My first impulse was that of compassion for this individual; but on a closer inspection, I was led to conclude that the fever was the consequence instead of the precursor of the brandy, and that dread of punishment had rendered the man vociferous.

We entered now into consideration how this odd-looking article could be conveyed to the tent, in order to be placed under the surgeon's hands; when just in the nick of time a huge empty rum-cask floated by: we caught it, poured out the water, and popped therein the linen man; and as companions of his voyage, we put in likewise a cage containing three live canary-birds, which latter formed subsequently the only provision during a whole day for three men. A pig also, which had just come floating by upon the lid of a chest, trembling violently all over, was taken in tow immediately: on this lid I read, with considerable surprise, my own name; which gave me abundant reason to suspect that my chest had been plundered by some good friend or other.

Ten of the party now set out on their way home, loaded with sundry articles of utility. I had the charge of my friend in the grog-tub, which I sometimes shoved before me, and sometimes drew along with a rope—and which, in short, proved to me a very great source of annoyance. Another man attended the floating pig behind; and was followed by three or four sailors, dragging through the water three live pigs and two live sheep, saved from the wreck; the remainder, loaded with drowned fowls, pistols, muskets, &c. closed the procession.

Besides what I have related, nothing particular occurred during this day's expedition, excepting that a little jealousy at times broke out amongst the party—a dangerous feeling under such circumstances of jeopardy. My convoy in the cask were all of them exceedingly noisy, each after his own fashion, during the passage homewards—especially the human biped, who screamed out eternally about his broken leg, his thirst, his bad food, and, though last not least, about his wet seat: to remedy the latter evil, we supplied him with a broken bottle, wherewith to lade out the water; but his actions being of rather an unsteady cast, he frequently lost his equilibrium in the attempt, on which occasions the briny liquid rushed in, in great quantities.

About five o'clock in the evening, we arrived, greatly fatigued, upon the sand-bank, and were received, together with our booty, with acclamations of joy and welcome. The grog-coop was dragged on the sand with a loud outcry; the patient taken out very carefully, and borne to the tent by the third officer and some sailors, who laid him down before the doctor, after having received frequent cautions to this effect: "Ease me down gently! Take care of my left leg!" When the surgeon first perceived the state in which his patient was, he expressed considerable surprise at the immensity of the tumour, and was not without dread of mortification, which rendered the patient exceedingly uneasy. The muslin, however, having been, piece by piece, unrolled, it was discovered that the leg was neither fractured nor dislocated: the surgeon assuring us that it was nothing but a very unimportant contusion. My friend now grew quite angry; declaring, with an oath, that his leg was, and must be, broken.

Suddenly, whilst engaged in making speculation on this interesting subject, and quizzing the half-drunken invalid, we heard several loud hurras uplifted on the shore; towards which all immediately hastened, leaving the broken-legged gentleman to hobble after us as well as he could, or abide behind, which latter course he preferred. These cheers proceeded from the chief officer and his party, who were returned from the wreck with the large cutter, after having hauled her three miles, with inexpressible labour, over the rocks and sand:—we gave three cheers in return, and triumphantly hauled the boat upon the beach, close to the tent, in readiness for the carpenter to commence his repairs.

We now proceeded, about six o'clock in the evening, to take our meal, which consisted of a cup of beer, and a small portion of drowned fowl, to each man. This latter was divided with the greatest fairness, the average quantity amounting to no more than half a leg or half a wing: but on the whole we found our situation a good deal improved. Our provisions at present comprised six young live pigs, five live sheep, fifty pieces of pork and beef, twenty-four drowned fowls, three casks of beer, four dozen of wine, and one dozen of cherry brandy, a little keg of flour, and fire pine cheeses: we possessed, however, neither water nor biscuit. Besides these articles of food, we had a quadrant and a sextant; the Guide to the East Indies, by Horseburg; Norie's Navigation; several guns, pistols, and cutlasses; a frying-pan, plates, knives, forks, &c. Those who had been on the adjoining sand-bank contributed nothing to the general stock but twenty pieces of salt pork. They all appeared to be pretty well by the head, and stated that several of their companions were left three or four miles behind. Farquharson, the caulker's mate, who had shown, at the shipwreck, a good deal of courage and intrepidity, but who not having been upon the coral-reef, was concluded to be dead, made his appearance late this evening, to the joy and astonishment of all, in our tent. This man had been, it seems, one of the first of those who came from the wreck upon the reef; and, without saying a word, had departed thence to the nearest sandbank, in order to find, if he could, a better place of sojourn for us. What he had to relate, with reference to this voyage of discovery, was not of a very consolatory nature. He had wandered from morning till evening, along a chain of low desert sand-downs, half swimming, half floating, upon a plank, and shoving himself over with a pole from one to the other. On the approach of night he found himself thoroughly exhausted, and, cutting open a bate of cloth that had washed up there, he made a rough couch to steep on, intending to resume his expedition next morning. When, however, at sun-rise he perceived no signs of habitable land, and nothing but low desolate sand-banks stretching away to the N.W. he returned forthwith, and arrived at seven o'clock in the evening, quite fatigued, in our tent. As far as he went, he saw various ruins of the lading of the ship, including, with the exception of victuals, all other kinds of things. His opinion was, that our sand-bank was the highest of the series, and therefore the best adapted for our purpose. An hour after our friend's arrival, an officer's watch was set, to observe the rising and falling of the water; to keep a look-out for ships; and most particularly to protect us from any invasion of our provender or other preserved goods. Accordingly, a large watch-fire was lighted and kept burning, and the guard provided with guns and pistols, loaded with pebbles and gun-powder, it being generally agreed on that they should challenge the first man whose step might be heard within five paces of the magazines,—which were established near our tent, and surrounded by a railing;—and fire immediately, in case no answer was returned.

CHAPTER 16

Mutineers

By constantly walking about without shoes upon sharp coral rocks, our feet had become blistered and full of wounds. We anointed them in the evening with brandy and pomatum, bandaged them in muslin by the advice of some of our suffering companions who had found relief therefrom, and then laid us down to rest. This night, in addition to other inconveniences, was cold and rainy; notwithstanding which we passed it in greater comfort than we had done the night before. By daybreak every man was ready to go to his work, except the sick and habitually lazy. The carpenter and his mates proceeded without delay to repair the large cutter: the sail-maker, whose bag containing needles and other articles providentially washed up on the sand, set to, for .the purpose of constructing sails: whilst the boatswain essayed to make ropes by twisting together three pieces of muslin; others went once more to the wreck, and others again to the different sand-banks. Another party remained ashore, in order to construct more tents, and, if possible, to erect a higher flag-pole.

Our chief officer was, this time, in command of those who proceeded to the sand-banks, whilst I attached myself to the party who proposed to visit the wreck.

We arrived at her side about noon, and found that the upper part of the poop and forecastle was driven about a hundred and twenty yards nearer to the rock:—probably the lower part of the hold had loosened itself, and remained upon the outer ledge of the reef against which it had struck. Upon entering the cuddy, which was still partly whole and out of the water, we found, to our unspeakable surprise, a sailor who was lying flat on his face, near an empty brandy-cask, fast asleep. We strove to awaken and to raise him:—but he was so much overcome by liquor as to be unable either to move or speak; and in this state we stowed him, together with some sails, tackle, and some dozen bottles of wine, upon a raft which we had built for the purpose of floating home any thing we might be able to save: seven or eight men piloted the raft back to the tents directly; the rest of us stayed behind, for the purpose of transporting the captain's cutter, which we were delighted to observe, although in a very damaged state, lying not far from the wreck, to our tent. We could not this time discover either biscuit, or other article of food or utility, among the ruins; and returned, therefore, to shore, trailing the boat behind us. On the way, we met with two of the revolted drunken party, who, at the time we waded by them, were engaged in a sharp dispute, themselves up to the middle in water. One was holding a hat filled with watches, rings, and other little pieces of finery, under his arm; the other had tied round his body a girdle of muslin, which was filled with dollars. The latter was desirous to bargain with the former for a gold watch. "I will give you," said he, "four dollars, Bill!"

"Go to the devil with your dollars," replied his friend.

"Come, here are eight for you!" exclaimed the would-be purchaser; who, not waiting further reply, made a grab in his worthy companion's hat, and hauled out from thence a whole fist-full, spilling a great many valuables into the water:—they now put, the one his hat, and the other his girdle, &c. upon a piece of rock which was above water, and each made preparation to decide the affair à l'Angloise, on the spot. We did not lose time in watching the issue of this wise contest, but passed quietly by without taking any notice, regarding watches and dollars as the most useless things we could meet with.

Upon arriving at the tent with the captain's cutter, we were received with loud shouts of joy and exultation. The carpenters were obliged to repair this with the same care as they had done the larger vessel. The first officer now returned with his party from the more remote sand-banks, bringing with him many articles of great utility. The provisions in our magazines were this day augmented by four butts of fresh water, four casks of beer, three dozen bottles of wine, forty pieces of beef and pork, and a half-drowned, half-rotten pig. Some sails and ropes were likewise saved.

When, about six o'clock, we took our homely meal, the officer related to us his adventures. He had left behind sixteen mutinous drunkards, and had found upon a sand-bank the corpses of five of our lost messmates, which he had interred. By the flannel dress of one of these poor sufferers, he recognised Capt. Dalrymple. That was the only point by which he could be known; since the head, and the fourth finger, on which latter he was accustomed to wear a beautiful seal-ring, were missing. We afterwards learnt that one of the mutineers was detected by another in the act of biting off the finger in question, that being the only way in which he could gain possession of the ring. All endeavours to regain this valuable article—valuable to us in various ways—were unavailing. The next day, Friday the 10th of July, the carpenters, sail-makers, and other workmen, were extremely active in fitting out the large cutter: a strong party also went back to the wreck, and another, as usual, to the sandbanks. Some were now set about making clothes, particularly trousers, from the Company's cloth, using twisted stripes of muslin for thread. Others began to try their luck in fishing; and others again stopped at home to repair the tents, and to prepare and cook the victuals. The chief officer and I resolved to wade this day, with a brave company, to certain sand-banks which were situated further down, where we thought it probable we might find more scattered articles than even on the wreck. We were obliged to pass the Beer Island; and after having waded for two hours, sometimes up to the neck in water, and sometimes over soft dry sand, we arrived there. How surprised were we! I thought we looked wild and uncouth enough at home; but upon getting a sight of these, I almost grew vain of our comparatively comely appearance. Their settlement was in the shape of a crescent, and consisted of about twenty large beer-casks, each forming the back part of a little tent, in order to be handy for tapping; which ceremony they performed by staving-in the head, and baling out the beer with a globe-lamp, or other similar vessels, in default of more eligible drinking-cups. They had very little meat, but were better supplied with fish, some of which they were, at the moment of our arrival, employed in frying over the fire. They were abundantly furnished with guns, cutlasses, pistols, knives, and other similar instruments. Most of them were quite naked, with the exception of having bound about their loins a piece of strong cloth, whilst a turban decorated their head. The rays of a nearly vertical sun, added to customary filthiness, gave to their countenances and bodies generally the hue of copper: each had a large knife, and a bottle of wine or brandy, in his girdle; whilst from his shoulder hung, fastened to a broad stripe of cloth, a musket, a pistol, or a sword.

Two of these personages were fiercely disputing about a beautiful fowling-piece inlaid with gold, and the feebler of them was soon knocked down by a blow upon the head—the victor triumphantly carrying off the spoil, and heaping curses and insults upon his less fortunate antagonist, who suffered so much from his overthrow that he was perfectly silent. Another young fellow, the doctor's servant, who was hunting after birds, which were extremely tame, and whose gun had been perhaps too strongly charged, had the ill luck to feel it burst, and inflict a severe wound upon his right hand. He cast down the weapon, and ran to stanch the blood in water: we took this man away with us, to place him under the care of the surgeon. Three or four others, comparatively sober, were occupied in fishing in the following manner: at low water they discovered that a great many fish were left in a little pool in the sand-bank, by the flood: they therefore, at that period, trailed a large piece of white cloth through the water, and caught more fish than they could consume in the day. At the time of high tide, however, their bank was quite overflown; so that only an interval of five or six feet was left between the tons and the sea; from which circumstance, the situation of these people was certainly more dangerous than our own. But the thought of being unrestricted in beer and spirits made them forget all disadvantages; and before our departure, their number had increased to twenty-five. They malted, in fact, to such a degree, that scarce one of them could see a hole through a grating: and no one could possibly dispute their title to the honourable appellation of Beer-Islanders. All their stock of wine and brandy had been hidden in the sand previous to our arrival; and as we were weak, and not very much disposed to fight, we could not make prizes of any casks of beer, and set out on our return without at all interfering with their property. To do them justice, however, they certainly invited us, with great civility, to drink with them.

We constructed a raft, of spars that we had picked up along the beach, and loaded it with thirty pieces of pork, three dozen of wine, and two little empty kegs, which we intended for the large cutter: this raft we dragged about a mile through the water, arriving at our own settlement about six in the evening. After the usual allowance of meat and beer, accounts of provisions and drink were cast up: four butts of water, five pieces of pork, and a small keg of lime juice, were the only articles saved this day from the wreck; and there appeared but slight hopes of getting any more from that quarter. About eight o'clock, p.m. the watch was set, as usual; and the orders for the night were, chiefly, to keep up a good large fire, in case of any ships passing by, and to keep a shrewd lookout for the Beer-Island gang, by whom a tremendous fire was lighted, until, towards midnight, it languished and went out, most probably in consequence of the whole party falling dead asleep.

In similar occupations and little adventures passed also Saturday, July 11. The great object of our exertions was fishing; fishhooks being made out of the inside works of chronometers that bad washed ashore, and nets out of thin stripes of muslin or Irish linen: with laudable industry the workmen still toiled in the repair of the large cutter, upon which depended all our hopes of final rescue from this forlorn condition.

By assistance of the necessary instruments, we ascertained the exact longitude, latitude, and name of the coral-reef upon which we had been stranded; and by the result of this scrutiny we found that the nearest inhabited country must be the island St. Mauritius, at the distance of two hundred and fifty miles bearing S. W. by S. Our plan was therefore arranged as follows:—as soon as the large cutter had undergone thorough repair, to send it out in this direction with an officer and some sailors, to reach, if possible, Mauritius, or Bourbon, or, in default of these, Madagascar. This voyage, in an open boat, certainly involved great danger and inconvenience: in particular, a compass was wanted, which could not be found upon the wreck, notwithstanding all the time and trouble we expended in seeking it, even from the first day; and there was now no hope left of procuring one, since the aft-part of the ship, the cabins, and the cuddy, were at length under water, and nearly washed to pieces.

CHAPTER 17

Preparing for Escape

Our tents cut by this time a very respectable and even gay appearance, with their blue, red, yellow, and black furniture, and amounted in number to seventeen; the officers, purser, midshipmen, surgeon, and passenger, who formed altogether our party, occupied the largest of these tents, the accommodations of which it may not be considered out of the way shortly to describe, in order to convey thereby some idea of the rest. It was ten or twelve feet high, and covered with red and blue cloth: two elegant globe lamps were suspended from the ceiling by stripes of muslin, and wax candles kept burning all night: in one corner stood a midshipman's chest, containing the nautical instruments, books, and pine cheeses; in the other, all our wine and cherry-brandy lay buried in the sand. Muskets, pistols, cutlasses, dirks, boarding-pikes, tomahawks, carving-knives, &c. were hanging and sticking about in various parts, whilst the sandy floor was strewn with pieces of cloth, muslin, cotton, or other stuffs. Little white jars of Naples soap and pomatum, letter-paper, pens, pencils, hair-brushes, combs, and a number of other useless articles, lay scattered about on all sides: Spanish dollars, watches, seals, &c. were scarcer, although frequently to be met with by accident amongst the sand, as nobody took the least trouble to look after them;—such is the idleness of finery or of wealth, when viewed with reference to their intrinsic value. The sailmaker and his mates occupied the fore-ground, busily employed in making sails for the large cutter: they complained of the want of palms, but some English half-crown pieces were discovered to be excellent substitutes. In the further corner sat Mr. H— the passenger, upon some bales of cloth. This man was generally called amongst us the child of fortune; since he possessed what each of us stood in great need of,—a pair of trousers, a coat, a hat, a snuff-box, and even a pair of shoes. The envy of the whole ship's company was excited by this immoderate opulence; and those who could command in abundance the materials of splendour, were smitten with the sharpest desire to exchange them for raiment any thing but tempting in appearance. It was the more provoking, too, as the sedentary turn of mind displayed by the owner of this much-envied wardrobe prevented him from making any great use of his advantages. In the opposite corner had our knight of the broken leg established his quarters upon the midshipman's chest, whence he took good care not to move at all, nursing his hurt with the most elaborate caution, and covering it scrupulously with no less than eight pieces of muslin. In the middle of the tent, which was thus occupied, lay stretched through the live-long day upon his back, another gentleman, who, like the invalid just mentioned, scarcely moved or spoke, except indeed when he could get any thing to eat, to drink, or to snuff, or any body to scold. He occupied himself constantly in reading; being especially fond of the English novel of Rob Roy: only it most unluckily chanced that he possessed but the second volume, the other two having been abstracted by the colonists of Beer-Island, who doggedly refused listening to any proposition for giving them up.

The people separated themselves into different messes, the same as on board, each mess having a tent of its own. We continued to serve out two allowances daily; one in the morning at seven o'clock, and the other in the evening at six;—each meal consisting of about two ounces of meat, and a dram of beer.

Our fourth officer was elected to the superintendence of the stores,—an employment which was productive of much trouble and responsibility, since there were constantly expressions of dissatisfaction and grumbling whenever the distribution (particularly of small-beer and meat) was made. It is but justice to this officer, however, to say, that his administration was distinguished by the utmost possible fairness and impartiality. From the earliest hour of morning until late at night, he was engaged in measuring and weighing the various articles of provender to be served out: he had, besides, charge of our live stock, which may be quickly summed up, consisting of five sheep, and a like number of pigs; the latter of which were fed upon pomatum and perfumed soap; and these articles not being very plentiful, the poor beasts had seldom a full belly. A bale of hay was fortunately washed ashore for the sheep, which were, like ourselves, put upon allowance.

The surgeon experienced a small proof of this fair dealing on the part of our commissary of the stores. He was, poor man, often sick and weakly, and rather indolent besides:—he kept, therefore, close in the vicinity of the store-master, to whom he very often repaired whilst that officer was engaged in the act of distributing the victuals, asking all kinds of questions—for instance, when dinner was to be ready?—what there was in preparation?—and, in short, whatever inquiry his stomach prompted him to make. The answers to these questions were, as may be supposed, always short and dry. One morning, when he perceived preparation making for soup in addition to the usual allowance of meat, he suggested to our commissary, or steward, that it would be eligible to dress a certain portion of it with the accompaniments of flour and butter. His advice was however taken very ill; the latter reminding him, that there were by no means butter and flour enough for the whole crew, and asserting his determination to make no injurious distinctions;—to the justice of which resolution the applicant was compelled to assent. A moment afterwards arrived one of the fishing-party, but he had caught nothing whatever. He snuffed up, however, greedily, the savoury steam of the soup, and urged by some inward impulse, exclaimed, "Ah! how I should like to be in Fitzroy Square!"

When our meal was ready, all assembled round the tent, and an explanation was now entered into as to the proportion of victuals which had been obtained by fishing or searching during the day: the scrutiny was, however, any thing but satisfactory:—to our misfortune, we had been singularly deficient in every kind of luck: no stray cask of provisions was rescued,—scarce a single fish caught. This gloomy look-out did not serve, however, to blunt our appetites. The slug soup was ushered in and devoured with prodigious relish; and shortly after, we heard from the front of the tent a loud "hurra!"

All started out of the tent, to learn the occasion of this shout; and it appeared that a sailor had dug a hole in the sand, out of which sprang, to his inconceivable delight, a fountain of fresh water. This news afforded every one the highest possible gratification: a pitcher was filled and handed round:—the supply seemed very abundant; and although the fluid, which was of the colour of milk, was impregnated with rather a strong flavour, it proved extremely grateful to the poor, half-famished wretches who partook of it.

One of the midshipmen, a youth of thirteen or fourteen years, making his first voyage, and who had attached himself to the party on Beer-Island, returned from thence on the morning of Sunday, the 12th of July, at the head of twelve of his companions, but quite in a friendly way: they appeared to have had some dispute amongst themselves, as most of them had black eyes, and wounds in different parts of their bodies; some rather dangerous, and requiring the surgeon's care. The lad gave, however, a very favourable account of Beer-Island: there were, he said, lots of fish, of beer, and wine; and one of the foretop men was elected chaplain, and read prayers every night out of a common prayer-book that had drifted ashore. The day appeared, so far as we could learn, to be principally spent amongst them in drinking, fighting, sporting, fishing, and cooking, and half of the night in drinking and fighting only. Our informant stated also that he had been there two nights and a day; his nightly lodging being in an empty water-butt, one head of which was knocked in, and the other turned to windward. He had slept herein very snugly, he said, in company with a certain black fellow, a most notorious villain.

As soon as this pretty youth came amongst us, he began to

vociferate, not for one breakfast only, but for two breakfasts and two dinners, as the allowance which he had lost whilst staying on Beer-Island! but on Mr. B.'s refusing to give him any thing at all, he walked off, grumbling,—"I know how to get my living, if you won't give me any thing;" and soon after returned with two fine sword-fishes, which he fried over the live coals, and made a very hearty meal.

No kind of work whatever was done today; and in the afternoon the people assembled round the large cutter that was standing close to the tents, when Mr. Ayres, the purser, delivered to them the following discourse:

"Comrades!—and you all my faithful companions in suffering! When we look about us; and observe our forlorn condition in this desert place, and bethink us how near we have been to death within these few days past—how the deep gulfs of ocean yawned, as it were, to swallow our exhausted bodies, and how miraculously we were preserved from the impending danger;—we cannot any of us be unimpressed with a sense to whom we are indebted for preservation from so many and great perils.

"Yes, my dear brethren! the almighty hand of God was over us. It is therefore our duty to fall down before him on this sacred day, to implore a continuance of his divine goodness and assistance. It is true, we have to lament the loss of our captain, who was universally esteemed and beloved amongst us, as also that of several of our true companions, who met death buffeting with the impetuous waves: but we will not quarrel with our gracious Maker: it was his almighty will, and the decree of his providence, that some of us should incur temporal destruction; and we will not presume to call in question why he has done thus, and not otherwise. Above all things, let us be cautious how we boast of having been saved for the sake of our own merits: let us rather submit humbly to the castigating hand of God, which will, I trust, lead us to penitence. We will sincerely confess that we are poor miserable sinners, seeking what is promised in the Holy Scriptures;—that 'if we confess our sins, God is faithful and just to forgive us our sins, and to cleanse us from all unrighteousness,'

"Therefore, my beloved brethren! let us turn to our Lord God with all our hearts; and so far from suffering our present affliction to be effaced from our minds, let us treasure up an undecaying sense of the mercies of Him who has snatched us from a watery grave.

"If it has been the will of Almighty God to throw us on this desolate shelf, he will assuredly not forsake us, but give us our daily bread, as he hath hitherto been pleased to do. Let us, therefore, place confident trust in him, that he will save us wholly from our present distress.

"It cannot be thy will, O gracious Father! that so many poor men, created after thine own image, and for whom thy Son, our blessed Saviour, has sacrificed his life, should perish; and much less can we believe, that thy providence (cut off, as we are, from our wives, children, parents, and other dear connexions,) will permit us to starve upon this desert island. May we, therefore, live together in concord and patience, and fully repose ourselves upon Almighty aid:—let no envy nor discord disturb our peace and harmony; and may we unanimously turn our attention to redemption from our present peril.

"This redemption, my friends! appears to be conspicuously placed within our reach. Let us not neglect or delay so bountiful a gift of Providence; but, by immediately launching our bark for a near and friendly country, where we may obtain assistance, insure the deliverance of all, under the divine guidance and protection. With entire devotion let us commit our boat to the mercy of an all-powerful God, and offer up, in spirit and in truth, with one heart and one soul, our supplications for a safe voyage: then, my fellow-shipmates! shall we be speedily delivered from this dreary abode; and never, I trust, shall we lay down our heads to rest, without an offering of thanksgiving and praise to that Divine Being who will have so benevolently rescued us from the very jaws of death.

"And now, my dear brethren! let our concluding prayer be that which the blessed Saviour has directed us to use when addressing our heavenly Father; and may his all-penetrating grace touch our inmost spirits with humility and sincere devotion, whilst together we uplift it to his throne."

Though a great many of us, during our prosperity, and indeed some even in the midst of these desolate circumstances, had much neglected worship, and thought indifferently about it;—yet on this occasion the most unfeeling hearts were melted, and the rudest amongst us were not ashamed to shed tears.

Chapter 18

Sailing

The following day we were so happy as to get ready our boat for sailing, and to equip it for the voyage; but not without experiencing many and great difficulties, being not seldom in want of the most necessary things, and absolutely obliged to collect together the pitch, from all quarters, in our hands: but it must be added, to the honour of our whole company, that every man fully performed his duty.

The boat was destined to be launched the next morning, and the names of those who were to man it were suspended at the entrance of the large tent, written on a sheet of paper in very conspicuous letters:—thus passed Monday, the 13th of July, in various preparations for our departure, and all was so arranged as to enable us without hindrance to set sail soon after daybreak.

Towards evening, I had a deliberative conversation, respecting the navigation of the boat, with Mr. Ayres, who always most zealously contributed to the general welfare, and had displayed upon every occasion extraordinary presence of mind and courage. We knew that the trade-wind blew, within about four points of the compass of S.E. by E.; and resolved therefore to keep the boat close upon a wind, till we had gained the latitude of Mauritius; by which means we expected to weather upon the island; and afterwards bearing up, and keeping her head due west, as well as we could manage to do so without a compass or chart, we hoped to succeed, under the guidance of Providence, in making that island. A quadrant, together with Norie's Epitome of Navigation, two chronometers, and a log-reel, were our only instruments and scientific means for accomplishing this voyage.

One of the sailors presented me in the course of the afternoon with a pair of trousers, which he had made on purpose for me, and which afforded me a great deal of comfort during the voyage. The provisions consisted of four pieces of pork, twenty cakes made of flour and water, one pine cheese, eight gallons of porter, sixteen gallons of water, six bottles of wine, and three bottles of cherry-brandy,—just sufficient to keep alive ten men for eight days, supposing we contented ourselves with the same portion which we had received upon the sand-bank. Besides these stores, we took along with us three masts, with lug-sails;—eight oars, some buckets in which to draw up water, and some spare rope made of muslin, in case of necessity; three guns, and some gunpowder; together with several bales of cloth by way of ballast, or to protect us in day-time against heat, and in night-time against cold.

Our intention was, in the first place, as has been stated, to steer for St. Mauritius; and in case we could not succeed in discovering it, we purposed to take our course towards the Isle of Bourbon; and should we likewise happen to fail respecting this place, to make sail directly for Madagascar.

Every thing being now in readiness for our departure at six tomorrow, and nothing left for me to do, as I was excused from keeping watch, I went to take a bath; having done which, I walked once more through our little sand-bank: it was eleven o'clock, and a beautiful night: I was quite alone, and in a solemn frame of mind.

To the north lay expanded the immense range of sand-banks, whereon, at a great distance, the watch-fires of the Beer-Islanders were just on the point of extinction: in our own camp, likewise, all was quite still, and every one fallen asleep, except the officer keeping watch, who lonesomely walked about the strand, and gathered pieces of wood, which he. threw from time to time into the watch-fire, the flame of which then blazed high up, whilst the crackling produced thereby mingled strangely with the noise of the foaming surge.

This latter presented itself to the eye, at the eastern and southern horizon, as a dense wall of water: sometimes I saw, through the high up-flying dash, the miserable remains of the *Cabalva*; and close by the watch-fire upon the beach lay our cutter ready for launching. The entire prospect sent deep into my mind the great responsibility of the undertaking of tomorrow, upon the successful execution of which depended the life and preservation of more than a hundred people.

The sky above me was quite clear, and lustrous with stars; the moon was setting in the western horizon, and throwing a pale shine over the whole surface of the sea. I fell down on the sand upon my knees, and prayed devoutly that the Great Spirit would look with compassion upon the frail destitute creatures now hushed in temporary oblivion.

When I arose again, I directed once more my attention to the course of the stars, and marked as minutely as possible the four principal quarters of the heavens: for should we fail in accuracy on these points we could not hope for any good issue to our voyage. I observed most particularly the situation of the southern cross, which was our only visible fundamental point from south to north; also of the Scorpion, Mars, Venus, and the half-moon, which indicated to us the eastern and western points. Having made my remarks, I went back to the camp, and lay down to sleep, once more recommending myself and my great undertaking to the Divine Providence. I slept very soundly and sweetly all the night, and the flame of the watch-fire was not yet extinguished, when I awoke more fresh and gay than I could have anticipated. In the east it already dawned, and I roused the whole of our company from slumber. It was a beautiful morning, and the wind extremely favourable. All were buoyant and lively,—un-subdued by long suffering, and full of joyous hope. Even the weak and invalid, including our friend of the broken leg, ran as nimbly as possible to the shore, to observe the circumstances under which we were likely to set sail; and to all was distributed, on this eventful morning, a better breakfast than had been commonly dealt out.

About five o'clock, as the sun was in the act of uprising, we entered our frail bark. All hands were in readiness to give us whatever assistance was within the scope of their ability; and thus the boat was soon driven from the shore into the water, accompanied by loud and reiterated shouts, and the tender aspirations of the assembled exiles.

We were now once more fairly afloat upon that element which had before displayed to us so much treachery: our cutter was launched on the western side of the sand-bank, and we set the mizzen and foresail; and haying caught the breeze, scudded swiftly before it, until we got clear of the breakers and outside of the rocks; but soon finding abundance of sea-room, we were aware that we should shortly lose sight of the sand-bank, and thereupon answered our companions with three hearty cheers, close reefing our sails, and hauling upon a wind. By the strong motion of the boat acting upon stomachs weakened through a protracted fasting of eight days, all became extremely sea-sick, with the exception of myself, who was fortunate enough to escape; whilst my hapless companions underwent dreadful sufferings, which proved a melancholy addition to the weight of our necessary toil and danger.

The atmosphere became soon thick and rainy, and so continued throughout the remainder of the day: we were hence disabled from making the requisite observations at noon, and were frequently obliged to take the foresail in, and heave to under a close-reefed mizzen. By the rays of the sun, which occasionally burst through the clouds, and by the current of the wind, we perceived that we were running in a S. S. W. direction at the rate of from five to six knots an hour. At sunset we were enabled to make a more accurate estimate of our course: knowing the sun's true western amplitude to be about W. N. W., we judged our true course to be S. W. by S.

We took our supper, each man receiving two ounces of meat and a little beer. A long night ensued, during the course of which no individual entertained a thought of sleep, as the waves constantly hurled water into the boat, requiring our most energetic exertions to empty it.

The weather cleared up as the night advanced, and I was consequently able to distinguish the most conspicuous of the stars. The southern circle became very distinctly visible: Its situation was 30°. from the south pole, and I accordingly reckoned that our course was S. S.W. We made four or five knots an hour.

With the renewal of day, the troubled state of the heavens altogether subsided, and the broad sun again shone through a bright and cloudless atmosphere. We knew that the sun's true eastern amplitude was towards E. N. E. and therefore concluded, from the present position of the sun and wind, that we were sailing S.W. by S.; and in this state things continued all the day, our boat making five knots an hour.

By noon, we were able to form very correct observations with our instruments, being obliged, however, to heave the boat to, in order to keep them from getting too wet. We found 18°. 50". southern latitude; the difference of time between the watch that was set upon the island, and the apparent time in the boat, amounted to about 5 minutes, or 1°. 45". longitude; so that we were 58°. 44". east longitude from London. But our calculation might not have been quite true, because our watches were wet, and therefore, likely enough, did not show the proper time. We flattered ourselves, however, every thing considered, that by this wind we should be able to reach St. Mauritius on the morrow; and therefore proposed to make, next morning, such observations as should be necessary, in order for us to steer in a straight course to the island.

We continued our voyage under a close-reefed foresail and mizzen, keeping the boat's head to the wind as well as the sea would permit us, which, in the squalls, frequently rose to a prodigious height, so as, in fact, to engross the entire attention of the man at the helm—the least negligence on whose part would have occasioned the shipping of heavy seas, and in all probability the swamping of the boat: indeed, the helm was obliged, during the continuance of the squalls, to be put hard down every four or five minutes, to turn her head to the mountainous billows which would have sunk her on the instant had they struck her side. It was really surprising to see with what activity she glided over the huge waves, which nevertheless kept us perpetually wet; so that notwithstanding our little bark was all right and tight, yet three hands were, without intermission, day and night, employed in baling her; nor were we free from alarm respecting the fate of our unfortunate messmates on the bank,—apprehensive that, during these squalls, the sea, as it very often does in bad weather, might make clean over the sand, and sweep them entirely off,—a fate to which, by Horseburg's Directions, we found several French fishermen had been devoted, who not long before had, like us, been obliged to take up their temporary residence upon the same spot.

As the sun did not set clear, and the night was boisterous, squally, and rainy, we could only guess our course, by the wind, to be S.W. by S. till it cleared up for a while at two o'clock, when, to my equal surprise and sorrow, I perceived, by the bearing of the southern cross, that we had broken off to S.W. by W. which occasioned us to fear that we might get to leeward of the island. Our rate of sailing, during the night, had been between five and six knots; but most unfortunately the log-ship was now carried away, with most part of the line, in consequence whereof we were compelled to guess at the rate of sailing, as well as at the course. This discovery of our real position was a cruel disappointment, since it tempted us almost to despair of regaining the ground we had lost; and we were actually upon the point of giving over all hope of reaching Port Louis, and bearing away for Bourbon.

Chapter 19
Saved!

The breaking of daylight on the 16th of July, after a tedious, restless, and altogether miserable night, inspired our little party with fresh courage and hope, notwithstanding the weather continued tempestuous and the sky cloudy and dark.

But what pen may describe—what tongue may tell—the sensations which agitated us, when, in about half an hour, we descried land gradually manifesting itself upon our larboard bow, and growing, as it were, from out the hazy horizon! A loud hurrah was simultaneously uplifted from every heart;—hunger, wet, the sleepless night, and the still more dreary day, were doomed to torment us henceforth no more! After this first impulse had exhausted itself, we sat for a few moments quite still, and stared vacantly at each other; some with clasped hands, or looks upturned to the heavy sky, calling upon their Creator with voices that struggled vainly for utterance, and words rendered unintelligible by overmastering emotion.

We soon became aware that the land which lay before us could be no other than Round Island, close in the vicinity of the Mauritius. Being a good way to leeward, we strove to work to windward as speedily as possible, and clapped the mainsail, close-reefed, on her; but the weather continuing squally, and the wind fresh, we were soon compelled to take it in again: notwithstanding which, we gained upon the land considerably, and found ourselves, at noon, abreast of what we conceived to be Port Louis, although twelve or fourteen miles to leeward thereof. The wind now drawing round to south, and setting right in our teeth, we were unable to obtain an inch of way by working to windward; we therefore took the sails in, got out the oars, and pulled for about the space of two hours: but the sea running high, although at the same time the weather was fair, we quickly found how little good was done, and accordingly set the three lugs with all reefs out. Evening coming on fast, our situation became alarming; for we were apprehensive, and not without good cause, that we should be blown off the island again, and thus be necessitated to stand on for Bourbon. During the pressure of this extreme anxiety, at about five o'clock in the afternoon, we observed a ship coming out of the harbour, running before the wind with all sails set. We immediately concluded that this vessel was sent out to our assistance, as our English ensign had been hoisted all day, union down, and we had every now and then been discharging shots. We sailed towards her with all possible expedition, and passed close by, under her stern, firing muskets as fast as we could load them, waving pieces of cloth, and hallooing to the utmost extent of our lungs. She proceeded, however, on her passage without taking the slightest notice of our various efforts to attract attention, and we lost a good deal of ground by bearing up for her.

We were now in fact quite out of our way; a disaster which would have involved the most serious consequences, had we not, by great good luck, got a slant of wind after sunset, whereby we were enabled to work in shore. We were however quite ignorant of the entrance of the harbour; and the night being, besides, rather hazy, we made a rope fast to one of the ballast-bags, and came to anchor, about two o'clock in the morning, in nine feet water, close under land, without having the slightest idea how near we were to Port Louis. The watch being set, we wrapped ourselves in wet cloth, and endeavoured to obtain a little sleep, notwithstanding the rain poured down in torrents. Two double allowances of pork, and one of cheese, two drams of cherry-brandy, a like quantity of beer, and two cakes, had been served out in the last twenty-four hours.

At daybreak we weighed anchor, and pulled the boat four miles close along shore; when, to our unspeakable satisfaction, we discovered the harbour, and got safe in by about eight o'clock.

As we passed through the harbour, the people of the several ships came running upon deck, staring at us with great surprise; and when we arrived at the landing-place, a crowd of persons of every description gathered round us. In point of fact, our appearance could not fail to have been at once uncouth and ridiculous: out of the whole ten, one only amongst us had a hat—the others wearing either muslin turbans or the ladies' fancy-caps before mentioned, made of cloth or leather, and trimmed with fur, and which could only be made to stick on the head by splitting them up behind: about three had sailors' jackets, whilst the remainder wore their sand-bank mantles of different-coloured cloth, with two holes for the naked arms: three also had trousers;—but as for shirts, stockings, or shoes, not one of either could be mustered amongst the entire party. Our legs and feet, and indeed the whole of our bodies, were thoroughly sodden with exposure to rain and sea-water; whilst our faces and arms had become so blackened by the scorching rays of an almost vertical sun, that, on the whole, we certainly must have looked more like Otaheitan savages than Europeans. The crowd was increasing every instant, and we were pestered with questions on all sides: let me, however, at the same time, thankfully acknowledge that the good islanders were fully as anxious to relieve our necessities as to learn our story. They brought us fruit, bread, coffee, grog,—in short, everything we could desire; and many of them even invited us to take up our quarters in their houses.

Mr. Ayres proceeded, without delay, to the agent of the East-India Company, to report to him our wreck and present condition, whilst I was engaged in securing the boat and seeing every thing taken out of her: she was then given in charge to the harbour-master, by whom we were informed that the ship which had so cruelly passed us on the preceding evening must have been the *Swallow*, Capt. Oliver, a free trader, bound to Bombay,—no other ship having left the harbour.

Capt. Oliver has since expressed himself very much aggrieved by such a report as the preceding, and signified his readiness to make an affidavit that our boat was not seen by any one on board the *Swallow*. The master of the harbour, as stated above, is my authority for mentioning his as the ship in question: as to the circumstance of our not being observed, I am at least confident of thus much;—that we passed, as already asserted, close under the stern—so close, as to distinguish the features of the men who were walking the deck. We made every imaginable effort to engage their notice; and in our desperation, could only account for such neglect by imagining that, from our uncouth appearance, they took us for a set of savage pirates, whom they thought the sea (which was at this time breaking over and knocking us about in a dreadful manner) would soon spare them the trouble of destroying,—or, if we were actually in distress, would prevent from telling any tales of their heartless unconcern, which, but for the kind interposition of Providence, would have been the cause of nearly one hundred and twenty human beings perishing in the most wretched manner.

I afterwards went with a French gentleman, an inhabitant of the town, by whom I was kindly urged to make his house my home, and who, in emulation of the good Samaritan, furnished me with dry clothes and clean linen. Having taken a moderate breakfast, (for after so long fasting I knew I should be very cautious with regard to eating and drinking,) I was extremely anxious to learn whether Mr. Ayres had succeeded in getting a ship for the deliverance of our poor fellow-sufferers who were left behind; and was overjoyed to hear, that the agent of the Company and the commanding naval officer had complied with all our wishes in the most prompt manner. Indeed, it must be stated generally, that in cases of this description, the British navy is always both ready and willing to extend succour, of which we ourselves received the fullest proof. Scarcely an hour had elapsed after our arrival in Port Louis, before the Magicienne, an English frigate, was in the act of unmooring ship, in order to proceed to the relief of the crew of the shipwrecked *Cabalva*: she was to be accompanied by His Majesty's brig, the *Challenger*. Mr. Ayres, two of our boatmen, and myself, went on board the Magicienne, to serve as pilots in case of necessity; the rest of our party remaining in Port Louis. We were received in the most friendly manner by Captain Purvis; and the sudden change from distress, want, misery, and anxiety, to a happy and comfortable state, produced such a peculiar effect upon my senses that I cannot clearly recollect the adventures of this day. Thus much I know, however;—that they led me into a spacious and well-accommodated cabin, where I laid me down in a warm snug cot, and fell into a sleep so sound as to wrap me in oblivion for the space of seventeen hours.

We had all Friday and Saturday stormy weather, so that most of our sails were torn, and several of our sail-yards fell overboard.

The account we gave of our misfortunes fairly astonished everybody; the events connected with the wreck were regarded as the most extraordinary ever known, and the officers never wearied of hearing our relation over and over again.

CHAPTER 20

Back to England

On Sunday, the 20th of July, the men that were on the look-out on the mast-heads obtained a sight of the breakers, and sung out most lustily—"Breakers on the larboard bow!" whilst the old French pilot shouted "Hard a-port!" These words had acquired to me a tremendous import:—the morning of the wreck floated, with all its fearful imagery, upon my imagination, and I thought we were on the rocks again! Fortunately, however, the sounds were not, this time, accompanied by danger; and having cleared, we worked in to leeward of the sand: nevertheless, had it not been for the intervention of Mr. Ayres and myself, the frigate would scarcely have found her way in, as the pilot appeared to be in total ignorance of the place. With the utmost joy we soon discovered the flag-staff of our ship-mates, then the wreck of the *Cabalva*, then the tents, and, lastly, the sand-bank itself. Captain Purvis saluted them with a gun every ten minutes, to which they replied by letting off large quantities of gunpowder.

Upon entering the bay, we obtained sight of the chief officer, Mr. Sewell, with eight hands, in the captain's cutter. The sea was at the time running very high, and we were apprehensive of seeing her swamp, but fortunately we picked her up safe, although in a very leaky condition. Mr. Sewell was received with abundant congratulations on board the frigate, and gave us a brief description of the events that had occurred upon the sand-bank subsequently to the departure of the large cutter:

"We repeated," said he, "our visits to the wreck, and the various sand-banks, in search of provisions and other articles of utility; but the store was thoroughly exhausted, and not a single thing could we procure. In fishing, we were more successful.

"The spirit of discord and dissension began to prevail shortly after you left; and individuals amongst us daily deserted, and went over to the Beer-Island gang. From these, however, we were sensible no serious disturbance would arise, so long as they should continue amply provided with spirits and beer; and, on the whole, they really behaved better than might have been anticipated, feeding chiefly upon turtle-eggs, which they caught in considerable numbers. The repair of the captain's cutter engaged our principal attention, and in her we proposed to make sundry little voyages of discovery, with a view to find, if possible, northward, a somewhat higher sand-bank. We also collected a great quantity of timber from the wreck, in readiness for the carpenter to build a flat-bottomed boat whereupon all our goods might be transported, if necessary, from one point to another. You and your boat were quite given over by us; since the weather had become so very tempestuous shortly after your departure, as almost to inundate our cheerless place of abode.

"We were assembled at devotion today, when the boatswain accidentally turning his eyes towards the sea, on a sudden interrupted prayers by shouting 'a sail! a sail! a ship, by the Lord!' and ran capering, as if seized with insanity, along the sand. The whole company instantly rushed towards the beach, cheering loudly for some time, and then dispersing in all directions with terrible uproar and confusion. Some fell foul of the victuals and beer, which they devoured without restraint; others set fire to heaps of gunpowder, by way of signal to the frigate; others, again, demolished in frantic exultation the now useless tents; whilst a remnant (I grieve to say, a small one only,) fell down on their faces to return thanks to God for our deliverance,—hastening afterwards to take measures for quieting the unruly, and attracting the attention of the frigate.

Amongst these scenes, a few men got hold of the captain's cutter, and made off with her into the sea. I jumped in, and shoved off with eight hands, leaving the people in a very riotous state—the officers being scarcely able to keep them from the provisions:—but I trust they are by this time brought a little to their senses again."

This night the *Magicienne* brought up in twelve fathoms water, weighed again on Monday morning, and in the evening of the same day came safely to anchor within a mile of the sand-banks, and right in front of the tents. A boat was now sent ashore, and brought back several of the officers and midshipmen of the unfortunate *Cabalva*. Both parties were equally rejoiced in meeting again, after this short, but trying and eventful separation of eight days. Capt. Purvis invited the whole of them to dinner, and they sat down in his cabin in their sandbank dresses, which had got somewhat more decent than formerly, although they still wore a very savage appearance: most of the gentlemen had trousers manufactured on the sand from cloth that had been saved; some wore a shirt, and one or two a jacket, which they had picked up about the wreck: but each man was provided with either a large knife, a pistol, or a dirk sticking in his waistband.

The evening was spent cheerfully, and even merrily; but a good deal of quizzing was discharged upon one of the sand-bank gentlemen for having overloaded his stomach with raw plum-pudding and pork-chops at the moment of the frigate heaving in sight: to such a degree, indeed, was he teased and bantered, as to prevent his sharing duly in the enjoyment of his comrades. The individual in question was no other than our old friend of the broken leg, and the following were the circumstances related. On the previous day, when the frigate was first perceived, Mr. M. beginning, in the midst of the confusion, to feel very empty in his inside, made to the store-room unobserved by any one, where the store-keeper found him almost choked with raw flour, suet, and plums, which he was mixing together in his mouth, and swallowing as fast as possible; helping himself occasionally out of a bucket-full of beer, by way of moistening the paste, and washing every thing down. The same

Sunday, it seems, happened to be his day for turning-to as cook, and accordingly, whilst the gentlemen were waiting for their dinner in the tent, he, without the slightest ceremony, consumed the pork-chops as fast as they were fried, until nigh half the dinner had disappeared. From this voracity, concluded they, not only did others suffer, but the gormandizer himself experienced the most undesirable results.

On the following morning, Monday the 21st July, Capt. Purvis went ashore, accompanied by some of his own officers, and some of ours; he took with him several bags of biscuit, which proved a prodigious dainty to our poor fellows, by whom they were demolished in a twinkling.

No sooner did the Beer-Island gang perceive the pendant of the *Magicienne*, than with great prudence they quitted their favourite sand-bank, and joined the other party. Owing to the humane interposition of the officers, no notice was taken of their misbehaviour: however, they expressed their sorrow at having left behind three casks of beer; and some few were even heard to wish the frigate at the devil, for coming to take them off the island before the rest of their liquor had been consumed.

The whole crew of the *Cabalva* embarked on this day: most of the men had concealed jewels and other valuables about their persons in the most ingenious manner; but they were so strictly overhauled upon coming on board, that every individual was despoiled of his booty. Subsequently, cloth, muslin, and linen were distributed amongst them according to their conduct during the shipwreck and on the bank.

Our chief officer remained on board the frigate, which continued here for some days, to endeavour to save some part of the cargo: the entire remainder of the shipwrecked people set sail for the Mauritius, in His Majesty's ship *Challenger*, on the 22d instant, and arrived safely at Port Louis on the 28th, the last of four eventful Tuesdays:—Tuesday, the 7th July, was the day of our wreck; Tuesday, the 14th, the large cutter departed from the sand-bank; Tuesday, the 21st, all the shipwrecked crew embarked aboard the brig; and Tuesday, the 28th, they all reached the Mauritius. Thus terminated our misfortunes, in a manner so prosperous and favourable as to exceed even the most sanguine of our expectations.

O, may every individual who participated in this great deliverance, never forget, whilst life shall animate his frame, the benign Providence which shielded us, even from the first morning of the wreck until our arrival at the Isle of France!

It is impossible adequately to express the disinterested attention and kindness which were extended to us by the captains and officers of the *Magicienne* and *Challenger*.

The crew of the Cabalva was afterwards distributed on board several vessels which lay in Port Louis harbour; and those who, whilst living- on the sand-bank, had vowed never to tempt their fate by going to sea again should they get clear from present peril, now unhesitatingly entered into fresh engagements, and were dispersed to all quarters of the globe. The officers and midshipmen were handsomely provided for by the Honourable East-India Company's agent; and most of them, after the interval of a few weeks, took their passage to England.

For my own part, I remained nearly three weeks at Port Louis, with my excellent friend and hospitable host, M. Pague, who, on my leaving his house, would listen to no offers of remuneration for all the attentions and accommodations with which I had been favoured: never can I cease to remember with gratitude the disinterested benevolence of this good man, to whom I was an entire stranger.

On the 15th of August, I entered myself on board the *Orient*, Capt. Barclay, a free trader, as third mate, and in this capacity made my passage to England, where we arrived on the 21st November.

I was received by all my friends and connexions with heart-felt joy; and when I communicated to the bereaved widow of Capt. Dalrymple the circumstances of her husband's death, I could not help feeling anew how much reason the saved remnant had to be thankful to God for their miraculous deliverance.

Subsequently, certain vessels with divers were dispatched to the Cargados Garragos reef, to recover, if possible, the sunken money-trunks, &c.: but all these endeavours, some of which involved considerable expense, were unavailing, and the entire loss was estimated at a hundred thousand pounds.

Such, in substance, is the statement of the sixth officer of the Cabalva, from whose account my own would not in the least vary. The Directors of the East-India Company presented him, on his return to London, with the sum of fifty guineas, and a sextant, upon which were engraved the Company's arms and a suitable inscription, and these gifts were accompanied by a very flattering letter. He afterwards became fifth, and in the year 1821 fourth officer in the service of the Honourable Company. Having made the voyage both to China and to the East Indies, he is, I believe, at the present time, at Bencoolen.

CHAPTER 21

The Rhine

Scarcely any one amongst the rescued crew of the ill-fated Cabalva could have any materials of import to add to the journal which was kept of our common experience, and which I have already laid before the reader. Should the latter however feel disposed, from the foregoing narrative of my life, to extend his sympathy to me, he will not, I am sure, feel uninterested by the little detail of my personal sufferings.

At that point of time when the first cry of alarm was uttered, on the fatal morning of the 7th July, I was most snugly nested in my hammock, and enjoying a very sweet sleep. Jarred by the scraping of the vessel along the edge of the rocks, I awoke, and the tremendous concussion which immediately followed threw me at once out of bed upon the floor, from which I endeavoured in vain to arise—the furious breakers hurling the ship from one side to another so rapidly as to render it impossible for me to regain my footing. A fearful cry was now heard from all quarters—below as well as upon deck; and I plainly distinguished the sounds—"Clear away the boats!"—"Cut away the masts!— Cannons overboard!" and other exclamations of a similar nature. I very soon became aware that we were stranded; and so powerful an effect had the sudden horror upon my frame, that I continued for some minutes quite stunned and senseless. At length I recovered so far as to feel the instinct of self-preservation, and gathered together sufficient presence of mind to look for my small riches, which consisted of some gold and a watch. I now hastened up the steps, a terrible stillness prevailing all around me, only disturbed by the sound of the hatchets, as they were just beginning to cut down the masts, and throw them overboard.

The utter darkness did not allow me to recognise any object whatever beyond the ship, and I stood transfixed with terror, laying hold, as it were mechanically, of the arm of the cabin -stair, to prevent my falling down. Perceiving me in this situation, a naval officer came up, and exclaimed:—"Why, you are turned, like Lot's wife, into a pillar of salt! come, come, stir about, and make yourself useful in some way." This rough but well-meant address restored to me my recollection, and I wandered from one spot to another proffering my services everywhere, but, to very little purpose:—nobody listened to, nobody cared about me; each being anxious only to provide for himself and for his own rescue. All our people were as yet on board, with the exception of a few who had been washed overboard, and were now desperately struggling with the waves, in order to gain once more the dismasted ship.

I scarcely know what I thought in these dreadful moments, for all my senses were confused and benumbed. At length it dawned in the east, and all the crew acquired in consequence new courage and resolution. The mist having dispersed, we were enabled to behold the continuous chain of the reef upon which we had struck; and when the large cutter was lowered, which took place upon that side of the vessel whereby I stood, I was amongst the first who leaped into it. When cast with my fellow-sufferers by the tremendous surge against the cliff, I found how valuable was the skill in swimming that had been acquired by me during my stay at Cabrera: in spite, however, of this desirable accomplishment, I ran a very narrow risk of being drowned, and should infallibly have encountered that fate, had not my better genius thrown an oar in my way, of which I took firm hold, although in a state of extreme exhaustion. At the same moment almost, a huge wave cast me and my oar with such violence against the reef, that I was left lying perfectly insensible upon the shore. On recovering my consciousness, I found that the oar, which my hand still grasped with convulsive energy, had stuck in a fissure of the rock, and thus the returning wave was prevented from washing it and me away.

I was fortunately saved from drowning; but the exertion and terror combined had reduced me to an exceedingly helpless and deplorable condition. I could not by any means collect my scattered thoughts, so as fully to comprehend the nature of our situation, in all its bearings: I stared vacantly around,—the objects impressed upon my visual orbs conveying no correspondent idea to my imagination.

The acute pain which I now felt in every part of my body, particularly my hands and arms, contributed more than any thing else to arouse me from this dismal abstraction: but I was still sitting and gazing with a stupid look of despair upon the scenes acting around, when on the sudden, I felt some one tap me on the back; and turning instinctively round, I received this salutation:—"Holla, Mr. German! what, has the devil brought you here too? Look, see, there, how they are crawling in the water!" My only reply was by a rueful shake of the head; but the good-natured, light-hearted sailor who had thus hailed me, continued, without changing a muscle,—"O! 'twould be all well enough if we could only get a little rum!"

"Tom," replied I, stimulated by this apparent unconcern, "do you really feel so little anxiety respecting our situation?"

"Why, what's the use?" rejoined he: "I should be a fool to think, just now, about future things; time enough, when necessity compels:" then suddenly directing his eyes in another quarter, "Look there!" he proceeded, "see that poor fellow swimming for his life: we must cheat old Davy this once;" and so saying, Tom sprang into the water as far he durst venture. I arose instantly, ran forward, and handed the lucky oar to my humane friend, who immediately extended it to the man who was buffeting with the waves, crying out, at the same time, "There, take hold of it, and don't keep me waiting here so long!" The grateful swimmer seized the oar, and we quickly trailed him to us.

After a while, the whole of our destitute company assembled together; and again did I find myself an outcast upon an uninhabited shore, and in a condition even more truly forlorn than when cast upon the island of Cabrera. We were here a fortnight; but during the whole interval, I saw scarce any one utterly discouraged—very few even anxious to any painful degree; and by far the greater number absolutely disposed to enjoy themselves as much as lay in their power, indulging the prospect of a speedy return to England, since the voyage to China was now frustrated.

Perfectly admirable, indeed, but scarcely to be described, was the general conduct of the seamen. After having waded perhaps from morning to night through water and sand, carried heavy loads, and received a very insufficient dinner, few of these resolute men manifested the least dissatisfaction; a steady seriousness, mixed with a half-subdued expression of banter, being displayed in their countenances; and jocular stories, relating to their former exploits, serving to amuse the tediousness of the evening.

It was curious to observe what a difference had been wrought by circumstances in the various objects of desire amongst the crew: the expression of our several wishes sometimes produced the most uncontrollable laughter:— one man for instance would sigh for an old hat —another for an old pair of shoes—a third for a neck-cloth, or some matter of equal importance,—which, under another aspect of things, would have been scouted as undeserving of notice, or actually thrown overboard in scorn. Some inveterate smokers, snuff-takers, and quid-chewers, were languishing in the most lacrymose style for materials wherewith to indulge these amiable propensities; and if any one amongst them got hold of a small quantity of tobacco, and was benevolent enough to dispense a quid or two to his messmates, he was immediately considered as a public benefactor. On the other hand, jewels, rings, and gold were absolutely despised—no one attaching to these the slightest importance:—in fact, a piece of biscuit would have been regarded as of much higher value than a purse full of dollars.

Everything which floated by, that appeared calculated to be of the slightest utility, was immediately seized hold of by us with triumph; and when a sailor one day found a quantity of shell-fish, he was received with a loud hurrah, the others running en masse to the shore, to seek a fresh supply.

When the large cutter had undergone a thorough repair, and was on the point of setting sail, every body was anxious to be of the party, and hence it became necessary to decide the boat's crew by lot. In short, the projected voyage became the universal subject of conversation, and numberless were the speculations put forth in all directions respecting its chances of failure or success; the chosen members of the little party feeling a sort of consequence spring from their election, and assuming airs thereupon which would have been extremely ridiculous but for the good humour with which they were expressed.

Thus, in a very short space of time, I underwent all the inconveniences and distresses of shipwreck, which, however, I was enabled to endure with tolerable fortitude, having been accustomed to so many previous sufferings.

At Port Louis I made the acquaintance of several residents of the place. Amongst the rest was a German, who had been for some time settled there, and, worthy man! had imported with himself, from his native country, the honest and social feelings characteristic of it.

I informed him that I had fortunately succeeded in saving my little money; and in reply he gave me not only good advice how to take care of it, but useful hints as to the way of increasing my store—clogged, however, with the irksome condition of remaining at Port Louis. I made some effort to reconcile my mind to this, but in vain: the longing desire for home was now grown too powerful to be restrained, and I could not meet speedily enough with a vessel to carry me to Europe.

From the agent of the East-India Company I received a handsome present of 100 dollars, and also a free passage to England on board of a merchant-ship. Anxiously did I long for the hour of embarkation: and when at last it came, I entered the vessel buoyantly, yet at the same time not without some misgivings, arising from the recollection of past dangers.

We weighed anchor, and set sail with favourable wind and weather. Off St. Helena we stopped for a while; and on the background of the mountain I descried Longwood, the residence of my old master, the Emperor Napoleon. I should have much liked to have seen that great, and in every respect remarkable man, but was not permitted even to land, much less to gain access to his person. St. Helena is certainly far from being the most agreeable place of abode that may be imagined; the vast unfertile mountains displaying no cheerful promise as to the productions of the island. Almost all the ships going to and returning from the East Indies touch at this place.

A short time only intervened before we got under weigh again; arrived, without any mishap whatever, in England; and disembarked at Portsmouth, where I found a vessel ready to set sail for Holland. I availed myself of this opportunity, and, after two days, reached Delftzye, passed through Holland, the Netherlands, and up the Rhine, until I came to my dear native town.

With a host of mingled emotions, well nigh overpowering utterance, did I enter beneath the shelter of my parental roof. Alas, it was so no longer! My father and mother were both departed to their long home, and my brother had become master of their old dwelling. I was received at first coldly—for at the moment my altered appearance failed to excite recognition: but a very brief space elapsed before the name of "Philippe!" was shouted out on all sides. My relations clung around me with fond eagerness, and reiterated their exclamations of welcome; neither could I, on my part, repress my cries of joy. My brother's family had increased greatly during my absence, and my sister had also, I found, united herself to a worthy and brave man.

The neighbours shortly after assembled together, regarding me at first with strange looks. In good truth, I must have presented a curious contrast to the youthful, rosy-cheeked lad they had bid adieu to some ten years before. My face was embrowned by the heat of a tropical sun; while long subjection to the storms of fate had disposed me a good deal to serious reflection, and conveyed to the lines of my countenance an expression of considerably more advanced age than I actually had attained to. Nobody could at first recognise their young acquaintance Philippe; but by degrees some trait of resemblance or other made itself visible, and soon all doubts were cleared up.

For a long period, my family had believed me dead, having heard the report that the entire army of Dupont had been taken prisoners, and I having never made any communication to assure them of the contrary. They had accordingly divided my patrimony amongst them; but it was without the least hesitation refunded, and consequently I found myself enabled to commence business.

A little while after my return to my native town, I became acquainted with the daughter of an innkeeper, and between this young female and myself a mutual attachment quickly grew up. We were, in due course of time, united; and several lambkins are now frisking merrily about, under the roof of the Golden Lamb,